basic crochet stitches

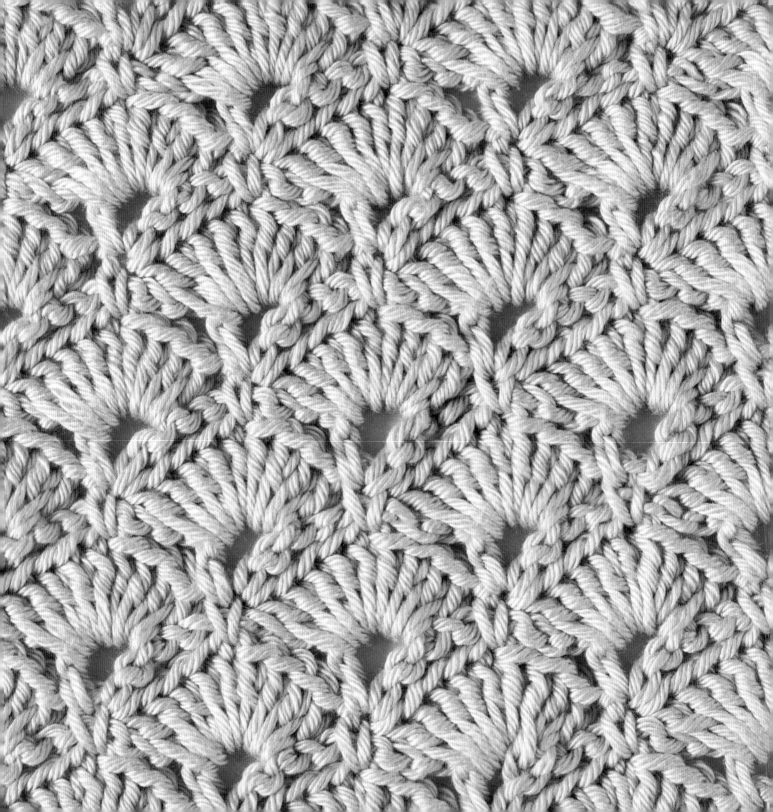

THE HARMONY GUIDES

basic crochet stitches

250 stitches to crochet

edited by Erika Knight

INTERWEAVE PRESS.
interweavebooks.com

First published in the United States by
Interweave Press LLC
201 East Fourth Street
Loveland, CO 80537-5655
Interweavebooks.com

Library of Congress Cataloging-in-Publication Data

Harmony guide. Basic crochet stitches : 250 stitches to crochet / Erika Knight, editor.
    p. cm.

 Includes index.

 ISBN-13: 978-1-59668-081-4 (pbk.)

 1. Crocheting. I. Knight, Erika. II. Title: Basic crochet stitches.

TT820.H27175 2008

 746.43'4041--dc22

                              2007038699

10 9 8 7 6 5 4 3 2 1

Reproduction by Dot Gradations Ltd
Printed and bound by SNP Leefung Printers Ltd, China

contents

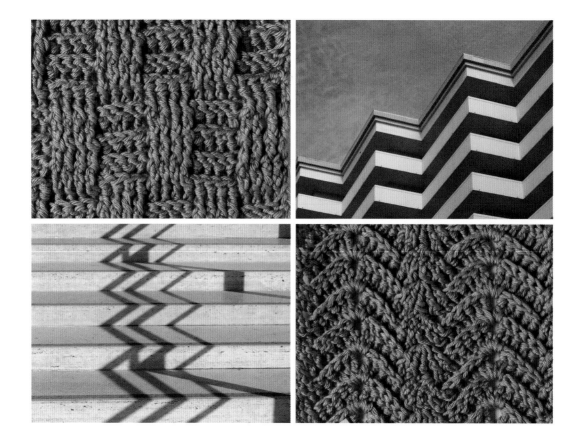

inspiration

The Harmony Guides are seminal resource books—each edition makes an invaluable contribution to the needlecrafter's repertoire.

I was first charmed by crochet when I saw the delicate edging on white cotton pillowcases, fine linen table cloths, and decorative anti-macassars found in thrift shops and yard sales, created and crafted by anonymous women whose proficiency and passion were evident in every stitch. But I was always wary of that little crochet hook, and just naturally preferred knitting—what I was used to!

All that changed while I worked in the Far East for leading fashion companies where a wealth of local craft skills and expertise was available. Here anything was possible, from fine, intricate, and embellished crochet to the more raw-edged stitches constructed in exciting new yarns and fibers from Japan. The women that crochet are skilled, quick, and creative, and it was a pleasure to work with and learn from them.

I soon overcame my initial wariness and realized that crochet is perhaps the most versatile of all crafts. Using just a hook and a ball of "yarn," it is possible to create a fabric from almost any length of continuous fiber: wool, cotton, string, ribbon, fabric, leather, wire, even plastic bags cut into

strips! Just keep in mind the intended use of the finished product, and choose the appropriate hook.

Quite simply, crochet is a series of interlocking loops of thread worked into a chain using a thin rod with a hook at the end. A chain of loops is formed, with each new loop catching the thread and pulling it through the previous loop. After the chain is completed, the thread is then turned to start a second chain, and so on, until a fabric is created— and rather more quickly than knitting.

Crochet can often prove to be easier than knitting, too, as working with just one stitch on a crochet hook at a time is much easier than handling a number of stitches on a knitting needle. There are only four basic stitches, too! Each is simple and easily mastered, and the variations and combinations of these are endless. This is why I was delighted to be given the opportunity to edit and contribute to this focused selection of basic crochet stitches from the seminal Harmony Stitch Guides.

I find inspiration for stitches and designs in many everyday things: the worn walls of buildings, patterned sidewalks, undulating tiles, the delicate stamens of flowers, even tangled and broken wire-mesh fences; seemingly mundane items, but inspiring in their form and design. I cannot resist returning to look at old, favorite stitches—the tried, tested and trusted—and also re-interpreting them. I have added a few more to this edition.

Crochet is one of the most basic forms of textile, having an affinity with fishermens' nets and medieval lace: the very word "crochet" is French for "hook." It also has an affinity with knitting; early knitting frames used a single, hooked needle, and it may well be that the looping effect gave birth to the crochet technique.

Designs were not usually written down, just lovingly remembered, and handed down from generation to generation. Crochet as we recognize it today became popular in the late 1930s and 1940s as a cheaper alternative to lace. Crochet soon adorned utilitarian collars and cuffs, and even snoods, giving femininity and a little glamour to the clothes of the austere war years. A revival in the 1960s took crochet to new heights, with colorful freeform hangings, even hanging chairs, and of course the quintessential crochet mini dress!

Once again crochet—with a twist—is a favorite with the designers of clothing, accessories, jewelry, even furniture, and other home wares. They are working crochet in surprising materials and colors.

I never tire of the varieties of texture of crochet. I like to employ simple shapes and combine them with contemporary colors and materials to create textiles that offer a visual surprise; mixing the delicate and precious with worn, weathered wood, for example, or robust stitched throws with the modern clean lines of a statement couch. And it is possible to create endless designs with just the basics of crochet know-how!

This edition is just a starting point, for your own interpretation. It offers a selection of 250 of the very best stitches, including a few new ones and some reinvented for a new generation. The guide offers everything from the basic skills and stitches, but also goes beyond the elementary to provide various combinations of beautiful inspirational fabrics to create numerous projects.

Crochet offers you the opportunity to create a very individual textile. It is so easy to carry around, too, you can do it almost anywhere—commuting, waiting in line, listening to music, reading, or chatting in a café. All that, and it grows so quickly—the best craft of all!

tools & equipment

It is sometimes hard to believe that beautiful and intricate-looking crochet is created using only two essential tools—a crochet hook, and the yarn itself.

Crochet Hooks

Crochet hooks are usually made from steel, aluminum or plastic in a range of sizes according to their diameter. As each crochet stitch is worked separately until only one loop remains on the hook, space is not needed to hold stitches.

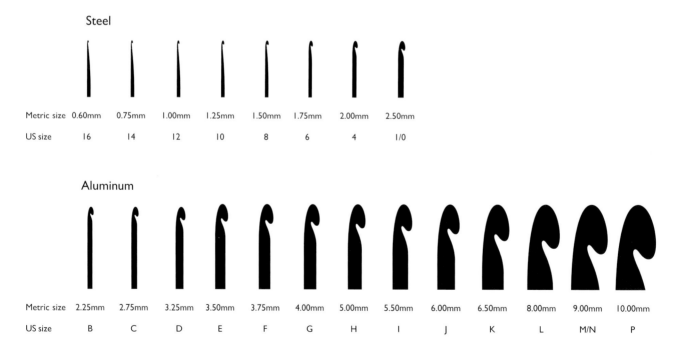

Steel

Metric size	0.60mm	0.75mm	1.00mm	1.25mm	1.50mm	1.75mm	2.00mm	2.50mm
US size	16	14	12	10	8	6	4	1/0

Aluminum

Metric size	2.25mm	2.75mm	3.25mm	3.50mm	3.75mm	4.00mm	5.00mm	5.50mm	6.00mm	6.50mm	8.00mm	9.00mm	10.00mm
US size	B	C	D	E	F	G	H	I	J	K	L	M/N	P

Crochet Yarns

Traditionally, crochet was worked almost exclusively in very fine cotton yarn to create or embellish household items such as table cloths, doilies, cuffs, and frills. The samples in this book were worked in a fine mercerized cotton, but may take on a totally different appearance if different yarns are used. Lacier stitches probably look their best in smooth threads, but some of the all-over stitches can be more interesting when worked in tweedy or textured yarns. Crochet yarns can now be found in leather, suede, and even fine jewelry wire.

Holding the Hook and Yarn

There are no hard and fast rules as to the best way to hold the hook and yarn. The diagrams below show one method, but choose whichever way you find the most comfortable.

Due to the restrictions of space it is not possible to show diagrams for both right- and left- handed people. Left-handers may find it easier to trace the diagrams and then turn the tracing paper over, thus reversing the image; alternatively, reflect the diagrams in the mirror. Read left for right and right for left where applicable.

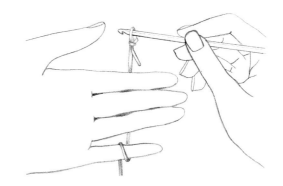

To maintain the slight tension in the yarn necessary for easy, even working, it can help to arrange the yarn around the fingers of the left hand in this way.

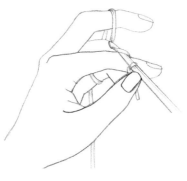

The left-hand holds the work and at the same time controls the yarn supply. The left hand middle finger is used to manipulate the yarn, while the index finger and thumb hold on to the work.

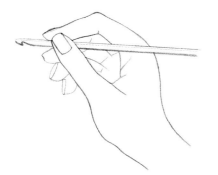

The hook is held in the right hand as if holding a pencil.

the basics

The patterns in this book use the following basic stitches. They are shown worked into a starting chain, but the method is the same whatever part of the work the stitch is worked into.

Slip Knot

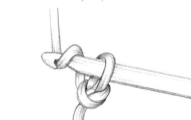

Almost all crochet begins with a slip knot. Make a loop, then hook another loop through it. Tighten gently and slide the knot up to the hook.

○ Chain Stitch (ch)

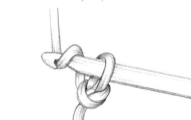

I Yarn over and draw the yarn through to form a new loop without tightening up the previous one.

Yarn Over (yo)

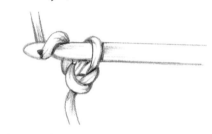

Wrap the yarn from back to front over the hook (or hold the yarn still and maneuver the hook). This movement of the yarn over the hook is used over and over again in crochet, and is usually abbreviated as "yo."

2 Repeat to form as many chains as required. Do not count the slip knot as a stitch. **Note:** Unless otherwise stated, when working into the starting chain always work under two strands of chain loops, as shown in the following diagrams.

● Slip Stitch (sl st)

This is the shortest of crochet stitches and, unlike other stitches, is not used on its own to produce a fabric. It is used for joining, shaping, and where necessary carrying the yarn to another part of the fabric for the next stage.

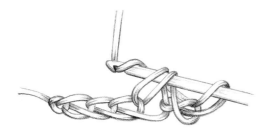

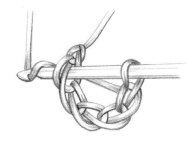

1 Insert the hook into the work (second chain from hook in diagram), yarn over and draw the yarn through both the work and loop on the hook in one movement.

2 To join a chain ring with a slip stitch, insert the hook into first chain, yarn over and draw the yarn through the work and the yarn on the hook.

+ Single Crochet (sc)

1 Insert the hook into the work (second chain from hook on starting chain), *yarn over and draw the yarn through the work only.

2 Yarn over again and draw the yarn through both loops on the hook.

3 1sc made. Insert hook into next stitch; repeat from * in step 1.

⊤ Half Double Crochet (hdc)

1 Yarn over and insert the hook into the work (third chain from hook on starting chain).

2 *Yarn over and draw through the work only.

3 Yarn over again and draw through all three loops on the hook.

4 1hdc made. Yarn over, insert hook into next stitch; repeat from * in step 2.

⊤ Double Crochet (dc)

1 Yarn over and insert the hook into the work (fourth chain from hook on starting chain).

2 *Yarn over and draw through the work only.

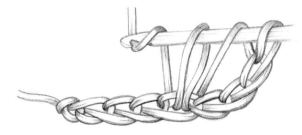

3 Yarn over and draw through the first two loops only.

4 Yarn over and draw through the last two loops on the hook.

5 1dc made. Yarn over, insert hook into next stitch; repeat from * in step 2.

$\overline{\mathrm{T}}$ Treble (tr)

1 Yarn over twice, insert the hook into the work (fifth chain from hook on starting chain).

2 *Yarn over and draw through the work only.

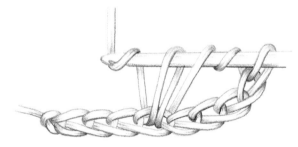

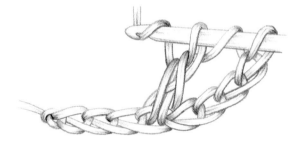

3 Yarn over again and draw through the first two loops only.

4 Yarn over again and draw through the next two loops only.

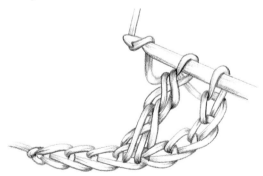

5 Yarn over again and draw through the last two loops on the hook.

6 1tr made. Yarn over twice, insert hook into next stitch; repeat from * in step 2.

Longer Basic Stitches

Double treble (dtr), triple treble (ttr), and quadruple treble (quadtr) are made by wrapping the yarn over three, four, or five times at the beginning and finishing as for a treble, repeating step 4 until two loops remain on hook, and finish with step 5.

Solomon's Knot

A Solomon's Knot is a lengthened chain stitch locked with a single crochet stitch worked into its back loop.

1 Make 1 chain and lengthen the loop as required. Wrap the yarn over the hook.

2 Draw through loop on the hook, keeping the single back thread of this long chain separate from the 2 front threads.

3 Insert hook under the single back thread. Wrap the yarn over the hook.

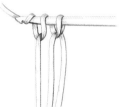

4 Draw a loop through and wrap again.

5 Draw through both loops on the hook to complete.

6 It is necessary to work back into the "knots" between the lengthened chains in order to make the classic Solomon's Knot fabric.

making fabric

These are the basic procedures for making crochet fabrics—the things that crochet patterns sometimes assume you know. These principles can be applied to all the patterns in this book.

Starting Chain

To make a flat fabric worked in rows, you must begin with a starting chain. The length of the starting chain is the number of stitches needed for the first row of fabric plus the number of chains needed to get to the correct height of the stitches to be used in the first row. All the patterns in this book indicate the length of starting chain required to work one repeat of the design.

Working in Rows

A flat fabric can be produced by turning the work at the end of each row. Right-handers work from right to left and left-handers from left to right. One or more chains must be worked at the beginning of each row to bring the hook up to the height of the first stitch in the row. The number of chains used for turning depends upon the height of the stitch they are to match:

    single crochet = 1 chain

    half double crochet = 2 chains

    double crochet = 3 chains

    treble = 4 chains

    When working half double crochet or longer stitche the

turning chain takes the place of the first stitch. Where one chain is worked at the beginning of a row starting with single crochet, it is usually for height only and is in addition to the first stitch.

Basic dc Fabric

Make a starting chain of the required length plus two chains. Work one double crochet into fourth chain from hook. The three chains at the beginning of the row form the first double crochet. Work one double crochet into the next and every chain to the end of the row.

    At the end of each row, turn the work so that another row can be worked across the top of the previous one. It does not matter which way the work is turned, but be consistent. Make three chains for turning. These turning chains will count as the first double crochet.

Skip the first double crochet in the previous row, work a double crochet into the top of the next and every double crochet including the last double crochet in row, then work a double crochet into the third of three chains at the beginning of the previous row.

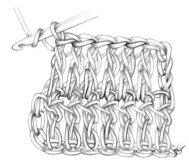

Fastening Off

To fasten off the yarn permanently, break off the yarn about 2 in. (5 cm) away from the work (longer if you need to sew pieces together). Draw the end through the loop on the hook and tighten gently.

Joining in New Yarn and Changing Color

When joining in a new yarn or changing color, work in the old yarn until two loops of the last stitch remain in the old yarn or color. Use the new color or yarn to complete the stitch.

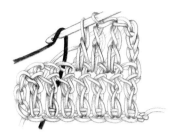

Continue to work the following stitches in the new color or yarn, as before.

If you are working whole rows in different colors, make the change during the last stitch in the previous row, so the new color for the next row is ready to work the turning chain.

Do not cut off any yarns that will be needed again later at the same edge, but continue to use them as required, leaving an unbroken "float" thread up the side of the fabric.

If, at the end of a row, the pattern requires you to return to the beginning of the same row without turning and to work another row in a different color in the same direction, complete the first row in the old color and fasten off by lengthening the final loop on the hook, passing the whole ball through it and gently tighten again. That yarn is now available if you need to rejoin it later at this edge. (If not, cut it.)

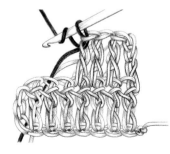

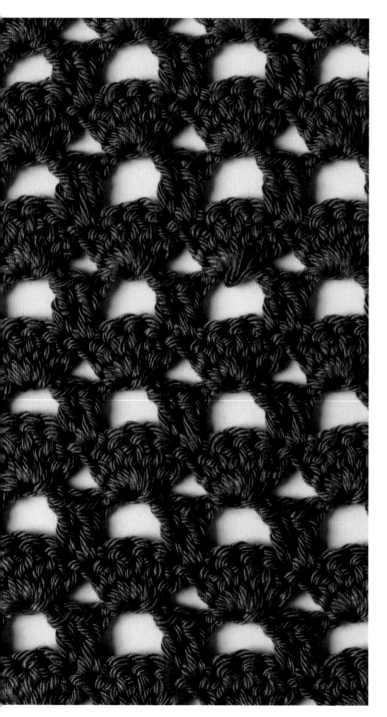

Placement of Stitches

All crochet stitches (except chains) require the hook to be inserted into existing work. It has already been shown how to work into a chain and into the top of a stitch, however; stitches can also be worked into the following places.

Working into Chain Spaces

When a stitch, group, shell, cluster, or bobble is positioned over a chain or chains, the hook is often inserted into the space under the chain.

It is important to note, however, whether the pattern instructions stipulate working into a particular chain as this will change the appearance of the design.

If necessary, information of this kind has been given as notes with the diagram.

A bobble, popcorn, or cluster that is worked into a chain space is shown in the diagram spread out over more than one stitch; therefore on the diagrams they will not be closed at the base.

Working Around the Stem of a Stitch

Inserting the hook around the whole stem of a stitch creates raised or relief effects.

Working around the front of the stem gives a stitch that lies on the front of the work.

Working around the back of the stem gives a stitch that lies on the back of the work.

Working Between Stitches

Inserting the hook between the stems of the stitches produces an open effect.

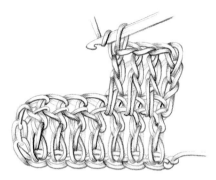

Ensure that the number of stitches remains constant after each row.

Working Under the Front or Back Loop Only

Inserting the hook under one loop at the top of the stitch leaves the other loop as a horizontal bar.

Under front loop.

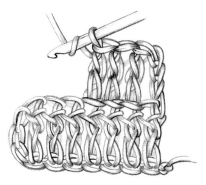

Under back loop.

Working in Rows

If you work consistently into the front loop only, you will make a series of ridges alternately on the back and front of the work. Working into the back loop only makes the ridges appear alternately on the front and back of the work.

If, however, you work alternately into the front loop only on one row and then the back loop only on the next row, the horizontal bars will all appear on the same side of the fabric.

Working in Rounds

Working always into the front loop only will form a bar on the back of the work, and vice versa.

Starting Chains and Pattern Repeats

The number of starting chains required is given with each pattern. It may be given in the form of a multiple—for example—**Starting chain: Multiple of 7 sts + 3.** This means you can make any length of chain that is a multiple of 7 + 3, such as 14 + 3ch, 21 + 3ch, 28 + 3ch etc.

In the written instructions the stitches that should be repeated are contained within brackets [] or follow an asterisk *. These stitches are repeated across the row or round the required number of times. On the diagrams the stitches that have to be repeated can be easily visualized. The extra stitches not included in the pattern repeat are there to balance the row or make it symmetrical and are only worked once. Obviously, turning chains are only worked at the beginning of each row. Some diagrams consist of more than one pattern repeat, so that you can see more clearly how the design is worked.

Working in Color

Capital letters—A, B, C, and so on are used to indicate different yarn colors in both the written instructions and the diagrams. They do not refer to any particular color. See page 19 for instructions on changing color within a pattern.

Increasing and Decreasing

If you are working crochet to make something that requires shaping, such as decreasing for the neckline of a garment or increasing to add width for a sleeve, you need to know something about shaping.

Increasing is generally achieved by working two or more stitches in the pattern where there would normally be one stitch. Conversely, decreasing is achieved by working two or more stitches together, or skipping one or more stitches. However, it can be difficult to know exactly where these adjustments are best made, and a visual guide would make the work easier!

On the diagrams below we show you some examples of shapings which cover a variety of possibilities. We recommend that you use this method yourself when planning a project. First, pencil trace the diagram given with the stitch. If necessary, repeat the tracing to match the repeat of the pattern until you have a large enough area to give you the required shape. Once this is correct, ink it in so that you can draw over it in pencil without destroying it. Now over this draw the shaping you want, matching as near as possible the style of the particular pattern you are using.

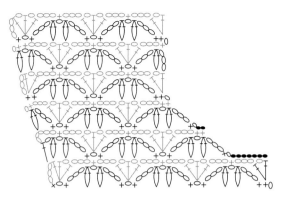

Gauge

Whenever you are following crochet pattern instructions, whatever form they take, probably the most important single factor in your success is obtaining the "gauge" or "tension" that the pattern designer worked to. If you do not obtain the same gauge as indicated, your work will not turn out to be the measurement given.

The gauge is usually specified as a number of stitches and a number of rows to a given measurement (usually 4 in./ 10 cm). The quick way to check is to make a square of fabric about 6 in. (15 cm) wide in the correct pattern and with the correct yarn and suggested hook size, lay this down on a flat surface and measure it—first horizontally (for stitch gauge) and then vertically (for row gauge). If your square has too few stitches or rows to the measurement, your gauge is too loose and you should try again with a smaller hook. If it has too many stitches, try a larger hook. (Hint: Stitch gauge is generally more important than row gauge in crochet.)

Note that the hook size quoted in instructions is a suggestion only. You must use whichever hook gives you the correct gauge.

Line showing required decrease slope

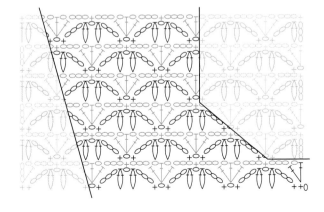

Line showing required increase slope

stitch variations

Different effects can be created by small variations in the stitch-making procedure or by varying the position and manner of inserting the hook into the fabric.

Filet Crochet

This is a particular technique of crochet based on forming designs from a series of solid and open squares called "blocks" and "spaces." These are more often used in crochet lace patterns made with cotton, but can be worked in knitting yarn.

To work a space, make 2 chains, skip 2 chains (or 2 stitches on the preceding row), and work 1 treble into the next stitch. To work a block, work 1 treble into each of the next 3 chains or stitches. When a block follows a space, it will look like 4 trebles; this is because the first treble belongs to the adjacent space.

Groups or Shells

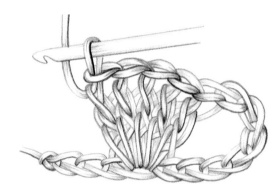

These consist of several complete stitches worked into the same place. They can be worked as part of a pattern or as a method of increasing.

On diagrams, the point at the base of the group will be positioned above the space or stitch where the hook is to be inserted.

Clusters

Any combination of stitches may be joined into a cluster by leaving the last loop of each temporarily on the hook until they are worked off together at the end. Working stitches together in this way can also be a method of decreasing.

It is important to be sure exactly how and where the hook is to be inserted for each "leg" of the cluster. The "legs" may be worked over adjacent stitches, or stitches may be skipped between "legs."

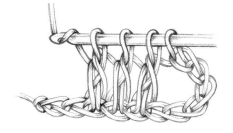

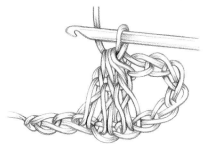

1 Work a double crochet into each of the next three stitches, leaving the last loop of each double crochet on the hook.

2 Yarn over and draw through all four loops on the hook. On diagrams, each "leg" of the cluster will be positioned above the stitch where the hook is to be inserted.

Bobbles

When a cluster is worked into one stitch, it forms a bobble.

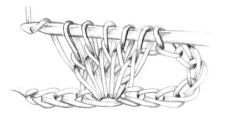

1 Work five double crochet into one stitch, leaving the last loop of each on the hook.

2 Yarn over and draw through all the loops on the hook. More bulky bobbles can be secured with an extra chain stitch. If this is necessary, it will be indicated within the pattern.

Popcorns

Popcorns are groups of complete stitches usually worked into the same place, folded and closed at the top. An extra chain can be worked to secure the popcorn. They're great for adding textural interest to a garment.

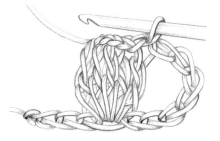

1 Work five double crochet into one stitch. Take the hook out of the working loop and insert it into the top of the first double crochet made, from front to back.

2 Pick up the working loop and draw this through to close the popcorn. If required, work one chain to secure the popcorn. On diagrams, the point at the base of the popcorn will be positioned above the space or stitch where it is to be worked.

Puff Stitches

These are similar to bobbles but worked using half double crochet. As half double crochet cannot be worked until one loop remains on the hook, the stitches are not closed until the required number have been worked.

1 Yarn over, insert the hook, yarn over again and draw a loop through (three loops on the hook).

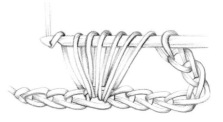

2 Repeat this step twice more, inserting the hook into the same stitch (seven loops on the hook); yarn over and draw through all the loops on the hook.

3 As with popcorns and bulky bobbles, an extra chain stitch is often used to secure the puff stitch firmly. This will be indicated within the pattern if necessary.

A **cluster** of half double crochet stitches is worked in the same way as a puff stitch but each "leg" is worked where indicated.

When working a large piece, it is sensible to start with more chains than necessary as it is simple to undo the extra chains if you have miscounted.

Picots

A picot is normally a chain loop formed into a closed ring by a slip stitch or single crochet. The number of chains in a picot can vary. When working a picot closed with a slip stitch at the top of a chain arch, the picot will not appear central unless an extra chain is worked after the slip stitch.

1 Work four chains.

2 Into fourth chain from hook work a slip stitch to close.

3 Continue working chains or required stitch.

Crossed Stitches

This method produces stitches that are not entangled with each other and so maintain a clear "X" shape.

1 Skip two stitches and work the first treble into next stitch. Work one chain, then work second treble into first of skipped stitches, taking the hook behind the first treble before inserting. See individual pattern instructions for variations on crossed stitch.

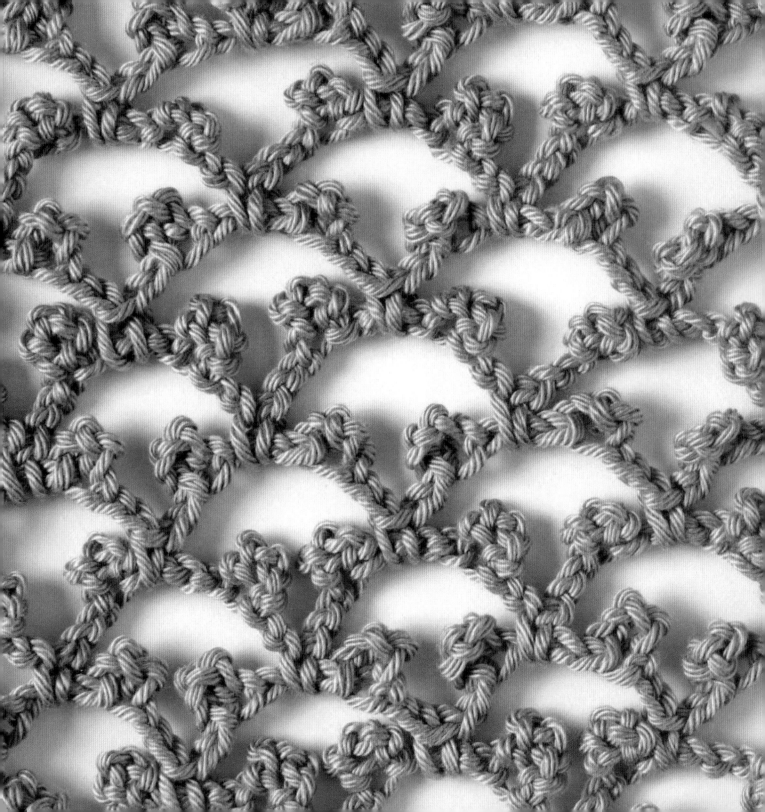

stitch gallery

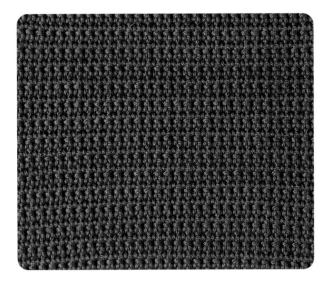

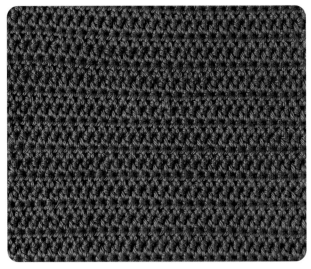

Basic Single Crochet

Any number of sts.

(add 1 for base chain)

1st row: Skip 1ch, 1sc into next and each ch to end, turn.

2nd row: 1ch, 1sc into first and each st to end, turn.

Rep 2nd row.

Basic Half Double Crochet

Any number of sts.

(add 1 for base chain)

1st row: Skip 2ch (count as 1hdc), 1hdc into next and each ch to end, turn.

2nd row: 2ch (count as 1hdc), skip 1 st, 1hdc into next and each st to end working last st into top of tch, turn.

Rep 2nd row.

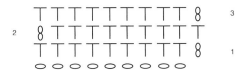

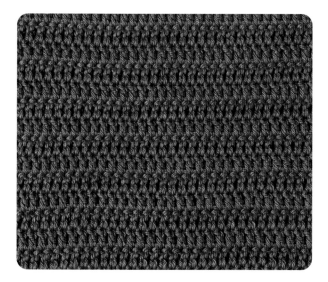

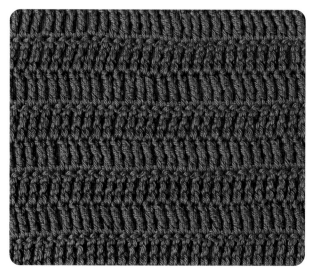

Basic Double Crochet

Any number of sts.

(add 2 for base chain)

1st row: Skip 3ch (count as 1dc), 1dc into next and each ch to end, turn.

2nd row: 3ch (count as 1dc), skip 1 st, 1dc into next and each st to end working last st into top of tch, turn.

Rep 2nd row.

Basic Trebles

Any number of sts.

(add 3 for base chain)

1st row: Skip 4ch (count as 1tr), 1tr into next and each ch to end, turn.

2nd row: 4ch (count as 1tr), skip 1 st, 1tr into next and each st to end, working last st into top of tch, turn.

Rep 2nd row.

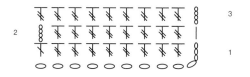

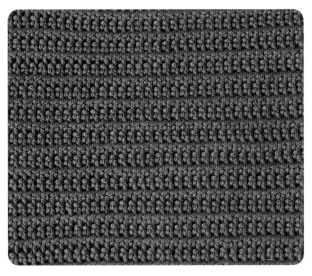

Back Loop Single Crochet

Work as Basic Single Crochet (page 32), but from 2nd row insert hook into back loop only of each st.

Front Loop Single Crochet

Work as Basic Single Crochet (page 32), but from 2nd row insert hook into front loop only of each st.

Back and Front Loop Single Crochet

Multiple of 2 sts.

(add 1 for base chain)

1st row: Skip 1ch, 1sc into next and each ch to end, turn.

2nd row: 1ch, 1sc into back loop only of first st, 1sc into front loop only of next st, *1sc into back loop only of next st, 1sc into front loop only of next st; rep from * to end, turn.

Rep 2nd row.

Shallow Single Crochet

Work as Basic Single Crochet (page 32), but from 2nd row insert hook low into body of each st, below 3 horizontal loops, and between 2 vertical threads.

Back Loop Half Double Crochet

Work as Basic Half Double Crochet (page 32), but from 2nd row insert hook into back loop only of each st.

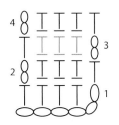

Back and Front Loop Half Double Crochet

Multiple of 2 sts.

(add 1 for base chain)

1st row: Skip 2ch (count as 1hdc), 1hdc into next and each ch to end, turn.

2nd row: 2ch (counts as 1hdc), skip 1 st, *1hdc into back loop only of next st, 1hdc into front loop only of next st; rep from * ending 1hdc into top of tch, turn.

Rep 2nd row.

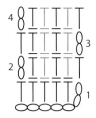

Wattle Stitch

Multiple of 3 sts + 2.

(add 1 for base chain)

1st row: Skip 2ch (count as 1sc), *work [1sc, 1ch, 1dc] into next ch, skip 2ch; rep from * ending 1sc into last ch, turn.

2nd row: 1ch (counts as 1sc), skip first sc and next dc, *work [1sc, 1ch, 1dc] into next ch sp, skip 1sc and 1dc; rep from * ending with [1sc, 1ch, 1dc] into last ch sp, skip next sc, 1sc into top of tch, turn.

Rep 2nd row.

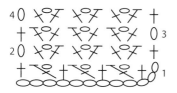

Simple Marguerite Stitch

Multiple of 2 sts + 1.

(add 2 for base chain)

Special Abbreviation: M3C (Marguerite Cluster with 3 spike loops) = See text below.

1st row: Make a spike loop (i.e. yo and draw through) into 2nd, 3rd, and 5th chs from hook, yo and through all 4 loops (1M3C made), *1ch, make 1M3C picking up 1 loop in ch that closed previous M3C, 2nd loop in same place as last spike of previous M3C, skip 1ch, then last loop in next ch, yo and through all 4 loops; rep from * to end, turn.

2nd row: 3ch, make 1M3C picking up loops in 2nd and 3rd ch from hook and in ch that closed 2nd M3C on previous row, *1ch, work 1M3C picking up first loop in ch which closed previous M3C, 2nd loop in same place as last spike of previous M3C and last loop in ch that closed next M3C on previous row; rep from * to end, picking up final loop in top of ch at beg of previous row.

Rep 2nd row.

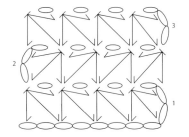

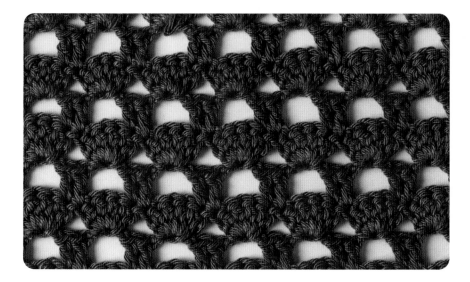

Boxed Shell Stitch

Multiple of 5 sts + 2.

(add 2 for base chain)

1st row (right side): Skip 3ch (count as 1dc), 1dc into next ch, *3ch, skip 3ch, 1dc into each of next 2ch; rep from * to end, turn.

2nd row: 3ch (count as 1dc), skip first st, *5dc into 2nd ch of next 3ch arch; rep from *, ending 1dc into top of tch, turn.

3rd row: 3ch (count as 1dc), skip first st, 1dc into next dc, *3ch, skip 3dc, 1dc into each of next 2dc; rep from * to end, turn.

Rep 2nd and 3rd rows.

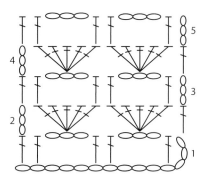

Multi-colored Parquet Stitch

Multiple of 3 sts + 1.

(add 1 for base chain)

Work 1 row each in colors A, B, and C alternately throughout.

1st row (right side): 1sc into 2nd ch from hook, *3ch, 1dc into same place as previous sc, skip 2ch, 1sc into next ch; rep from * to end, turn.

2nd row: 3ch (count as 1dc), 1dc into first st, 1sc into next 3ch arch, *3ch, 1dc into same 3ch arch, 1sc into next 3ch arch; rep from * ending 2ch, 1dc into last sc, skip tch, turn.

3rd row: 1ch, 1sc into first st, 3ch, 1dc into next 2ch sp, *work [1sc, 3ch, 1dc] into next 3ch arch; rep from * ending 1sc into top of tch, turn.

Rep 2nd and 3rd rows.

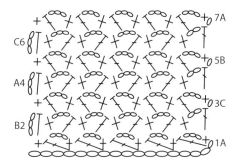

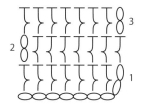

Linked Half Double Crochet

Any number of sts.

(add 1 for base chain)

Special Abbreviation: Lhdc (Linked Half Double Crochet)
= insert hook into single vertical thread at left-hand side of previous st, yo, draw loop through, insert hook normally into next st, yo, draw loop through st, yo, draw through all 3 loops on hook.

Note: To make first Lhdc at beg of row, treat 2nd ch from hook as a single vertical thread.

1st row: 1Lhdc into 3rd ch from hook (picking up loop through 2nd ch from hook), 1Lhdc into next and each ch to end, turn.

2nd row: 2ch (count as 1hdc), skip 1 st, 1Lhdc into next and each st to end, working last st into top of tch, turn.

Rep 2nd row.

Wide Doubles

Work as Basic Double Crochet (page 33), but after 1st row insert hook between stems and below all horizontal threads connecting sts.

Note: Base chain should be worked loosely to accommodate extra width.

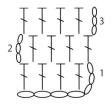

Herringbone
Half Double Crochet

Any number of sts.

(add 1 for base chain)

Special Abbreviation: HBhdc (Herringbone Half Double Crochet) = yo, insert hook, yo, draw through st and first loop on hook, yo, draw through both loops on hook.

1st row: Skip 2ch (count as 1hdc), 1HBhdc into next and each ch to end, turn.

2nd row: 2ch (count as 1hdc), skip 1 st, 1HBhdc into next and each st to end working last st into top of tch, turn. Rep 2nd row.

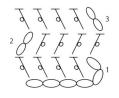   HBhdc

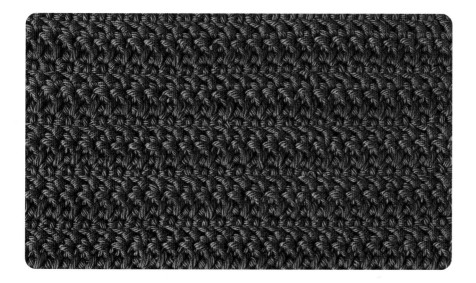

Herringbone Double Crochet

Any number of sts.

(add 2 for base chain)

Special Abbreviation: HBdc (Herringbone Double Crochet) = yo, insert hook, yo, draw through st and first loop on hook, yo, draw through 1 loop, yo, draw through both loops on hook.

1st row: Skip 3ch (count as 1dc), 1HBdc into next and each ch to end, turn.

2nd row: 3ch (count as 1dc), skip 1 st, 1HBdc into next and each st to end, working last st into top of tch, turn. Rep 2nd row.

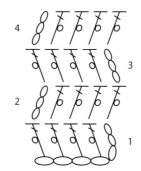

 HBdc

Loop or Fur Stitch

Multiple of 8 sts.

(add 2 for base chain)

Note: For plain loop stitch do not cut loops.

Special Abbreviation: Loop Stitch = Using the left-hand finger to control the loop size, insert the hook, pick up both threads of the loop, and draw these through; wrap the supply of yarn over the hook and draw through all the loops on the hook to complete.

1st row (right side): Skip 3ch (count as 1dc), 1dc into next and each ch to end, turn.

2nd row: 1ch, 1sc into each of first 2 sts, *1 Loop st into each of next 4 sts**, 1sc into each of next 4 sts; rep from * ending last rep at **, 1sc into each of last 2 sts including top of tch, turn.

3rd row: 3ch (count as 1dc), skip 1st, 1dc into next and each st to end, skip tch, turn.

Rep 2nd and 3rd rows.

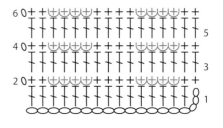

 Sc Loop Stitch

Ridged Chevron Stitch

Multiple of 12 sts.

(add 3 for base chain)

1st row: Skip 3ch (count as 1dc), 1dc into next ch, *1dc into each of next 3ch, [over next 2ch work dc2tog] twice, 1dc into each of next 3ch, [2dc into next ch] twice; rep from * ending last rep with 2dc once only into last ch, turn.

2nd row: 3ch (count as 1dc), 1dc into first st, always inserting hook into back loop only of each st *1dc into each of next 3 sts, [over next 2 sts work dc2tog] twice, 1dc into each of next 3 sts, [2dc into next st] twice; rep from * ending last rep with 2dc once only into top of tch, turn.

Rep 2nd row.

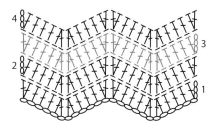

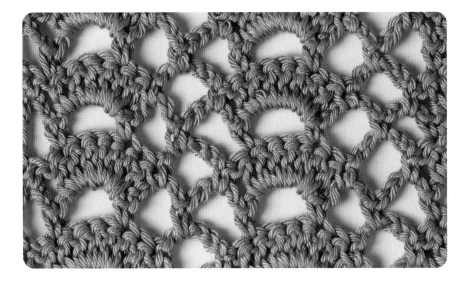

Fan Trellis Stitch

Multiple of 12 sts + 11.

(add 1 for base chain)

1st row (wrong side): 1sc into 2nd ch from hook, *5ch, skip 3ch, 1sc into next ch; rep from * to last 2ch, 2ch, skip 1ch, 1dc into last ch, turn.

2nd row: 1ch, 1sc into first st, skip 2ch sp, *7dc into next 5ch arch, 1sc into next arch**, 5ch, 1sc into next arch; rep from * ending last rep at **, 2ch, 1tr into last sc, skip tch, turn.

3rd row: 1ch, 1sc into first st, *5ch, 1sc into 2nd of next 7dc, 5ch, 1sc into 6th dc of same group**, 5ch, 1sc into next 5ch arch; rep from * ending last rep at **, 2ch, 1tr into last sc, skip tch, turn.

Rep 2nd and 3rd rows.

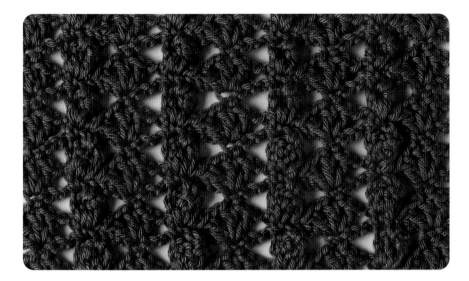

Global Connection

Multiple of 8 sts + 2.

Special Abbreviation: Popcorn = work 4dc into next st, drop loop from hook, insert hook from the front into top of first of these dc, pick up dropped loop and draw through dc, 1ch to secure popcorn.

1st row (right side): Work 1sc into 2nd ch from hook, *1ch, skip 3ch, 1dc into next ch, 1ch, into same ch as last dc work [1dc, 1ch, 1dc], 1ch, skip 3ch, 1sc into next ch; rep from * to end, turn.

2nd row: 6ch (count as 1dc, 3ch), skip 1dc, 1sc into next dc, *3ch, 1 popcorn into next sc, 3ch, skip 1dc, 1sc into next dc; rep from * to last sc, 3ch, 1dc into last sc, turn.

3rd row: 1ch, 1sc into first dc, *1ch, 1dc into next sc, 1ch, into same st as last dc work [1dc, 1ch, 1dc], 1ch, 1sc into top of next popcorn; rep from * to end, placing last sc into 3rd of 6ch at beg of previous row, turn.
Rep 2nd and 3rd rows.

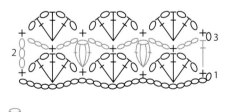

Popcorn

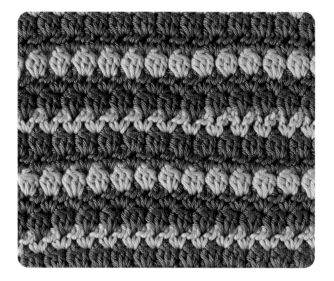

Zig-Zag Lozenge Stitch

Multiple of 2 sts + 1.

(add 2 for base chain)

Work 1 row each in colors A, B, and C alternately throughout.

1st row (wrong side): Skip 2ch (count as 1hdc), 1hdc into next ch, *skip 1ch, [1hdc, 1ch, 1hdc] into next ch; rep from * to last 2 ch, skip 1ch, 2hdc into last ch, turn.

2nd row: 3ch, 1dc into first st (counts as dc2tog), *1ch, work dc3tog into next ch sp; rep from * to last sp, ending 1ch, dc2tog into top of tch, turn.

3rd row: 2ch (count as 1hdc), skip first st, *work [1hdc, 1ch, 1hdc] into next ch sp; rep from * ending 1hdc into top of tch, turn.

4th row: 3ch (count as 1dc), skip first st, *work dc3tog into next sp, 1ch; rep from * to last sp, work dc3tog into last sp, 1dc into top of tch, turn.

5th row: 2ch (count as 1hdc), 1hdc into first st, *work [1hdc, 1ch, 1hdc] into next ch sp; rep from * ending 2hdc into top of tch, turn.

Rep 2nd to 5th rows.

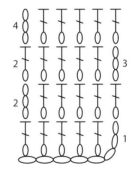

Alternative Doubles

Any number of sts.

(add 2 for base chain)

Special Abbreviation: Alt dc (Alternative Double Crochet) = yo, insert hook, yo, draw loop through, yo, draw through 1 loop only, yo, draw through all 3 loops on hook.

1st row: Skip 3ch (count as 1dc), 1Alt dc into next and each ch to end, turn.

2nd row: 3ch (count as 1dc), skip 1 st, work 1 Alt dc into next and each st to end, working last st into top of tch, turn.

Rep 2nd row.

Alt dc

Linked Trebles

Any number of sts.

(add 3 for base chain)

Special Abbreviation: Ltr (Linked Treble) = insert hook down through upper of 2 horizontal loops around stem of last st made, yo, draw loop through, insert hook down through lower horizontal loop of same st, yo, draw loop through, insert hook normally into next st, yo, draw loop through st, (4 loops on hook), [yo, draw through 2 loops] 3 times.

Note: To make first Ltr (at beg of row), treat 2nd and 4th chs from hook as upper and lower horizontal loops.

1st row: 1Ltr into 5th ch from hook (picking up loops through 2nd and 4th chs from hook), 1Ltr into next and each ch to end, turn.

2nd row: 4ch (count as 1tr), skip 1 st, 1Ltr into next and each st to end, working last st into top of tch, turn.

Rep 2nd row.

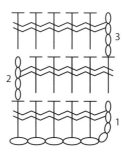

 Ltr

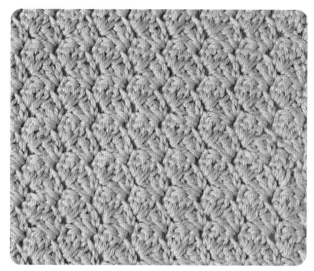

Sedge Stitch I

Multiple of 3 sts + 1.

(add 2 for base chain)

1st row: Skip 2ch (count as 1sc), work [1hdc, 1dc] into next ch, *skip 2ch, work [1sc, 1hdc, 1dc] into next ch; rep from * to last 3ch, skip 2ch, 1sc into last ch, turn.

2nd row: 1ch (counts as 1sc), work [1hdc, 1dc] into first st, *skip [1dc and 1hdc], work [1sc, 1hdc, 1dc] into next sc; rep from * to last 3 sts, skip [1dc and 1hdc], 1sc into top of tch, turn.

Rep 2nd row.

Sedge Stitch II

Multiple of 3 sts + 1.

(add 2 for base chain)

1st row: Skip 2ch (count as 1sc), 2dc into next ch, *skip 2ch, [1sc, 2dc] into next ch; rep from * to last 3ch, skip 2ch, 1sc into last ch, turn.

2nd row: 1ch (counts as 1sc), 2dc into first st, *skip 2dc, [1sc, 2dc] into next sc; rep from * to last 3 sts, skip 2dc, 1sc into top of tch, turn.

Rep 2nd row.

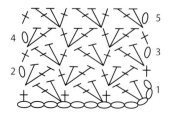

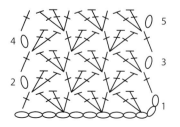

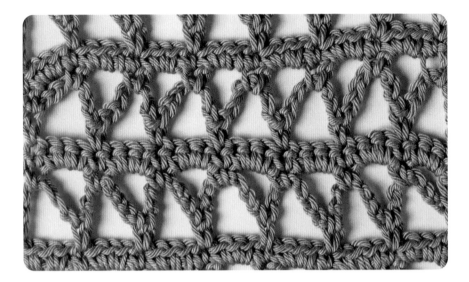

Ruled Lattice

Multiple of 4 sts + 1.

(add 1 for base chain)

1st row (right side): 1sc into 2nd ch from hook, 1sc into each ch to end, turn.

2nd row: 7ch, skip first 2 sts, 1sc into next st, *7ch, skip 3 sts, 1sc into next st; rep from * to last 2 sts, 3ch, skip 1 st, 1dc into last st, skip tch, turn.

3rd row: 1ch, 1sc into first st, *3ch, 1sc into next 7ch arch; rep from * to end, turn.

4th row: 1ch, 1sc into first st, *3sc into next 3ch arch, 1sc into next sc; rep from * to end, skip tch, turn.

Rep 2nd to 4th rows.

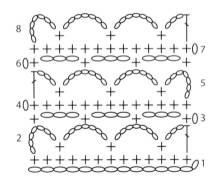

Fleur de Lys Stitch

Multiple of 6 sts + 1.

(add 2 for base chain)

Special Abbreviations

FC/rf (Fleur Cluster raised at front) = leaving last loop of each st on hook work 1dc/rf around next dc, skip 1ch, 1dc into top of next sc, skip 1ch, 1dc/rf around next dc (4 loops on hook), yo, draw through all loops.

FC/rb (Fleur Cluster raised at back) = as for FC/rf except insert hook at back for first and 3rd legs. Work 1 row each in colors A and B alternately throughout. Do not break yarn when changing color, but fasten off temporarily and begin row at same end as new color.

1st row (right side in A): Skip 2ch (count as 1dc), 1dc into next ch, *1ch, skip 2ch, 1sc into next ch, 1ch, skip 2ch**, 3dc into next ch; rep from * ending last rep at **, 2dc into last ch. Do not turn.

2nd row (right side in B): Join new yarn into top of tch, 1ch, 1sc into same place, *2ch, FC/rb, 2ch, 1sc into next dc; rep from * to end, turn.

3rd row (wrong side in A): 3ch (count as 1dc), 1dc into first st, *1ch, skip 2ch, 1sc into next cluster, 1ch, skip 2ch**, 3dc into next sc; rep from * ending last rep at **, 2dc into last sc. Do not turn.

4th row (wrong side in B): Rejoin new yarn at top of 3ch, 1ch, 1sc into same place, *2ch, FC/rf, 2ch, 1sc into next dc; rep from * to end, turn.

5th row (right side in A): 3ch (count as 1dc), 1dc into first st, *1ch, skip 2ch, 1sc into next cluster, 1ch, skip 2ch**, 3dc into next sc; rep from * ending last rep at **, 2dc into last sc. Do not turn.

Rep 2nd to 5th rows.

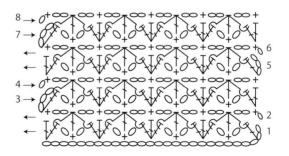

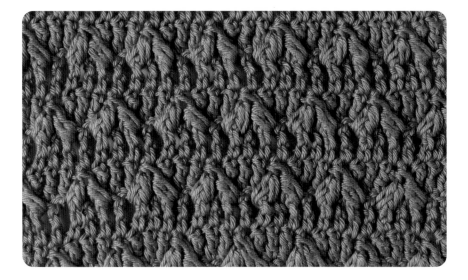

Leafhopper Stitch

Multiple of 4 sts + 1.

(add 2 for base chain)

Special Abbreviation: LCL (Leafhopper Cluster) = *[yo, insert hook at front and from right to left behind stem of st before next st, yo, draw loop through and up to height of hdc] twice, yo, draw through 4 loops**, skip next st, rep from * to ** around stem of next st, ending yo, draw through all 3 loops on hook.

1st row (wrong side): Skip 3ch (count as 1dc), 1dc into next and each ch to end, turn.

2nd row: 3ch (count as 1dc), skip first st, 1dc into next st, *1LCL over next st, 1dc into each of next 3 sts; rep from * omitting 1dc from end of last rep, turn.

3rd row: 3ch (count as 1dc), skip first st, 1dc into next and each st to end, working last st into top of tch, turn.

4th row: 3ch (count as 1dc), skip first st, *1dc into each of next 3 sts, 1LCL over next st; rep from * ending 1dc into each of last 4 sts, working last st into top of tch, turn.

5th row: As 3rd row.

Rep 2nd to 5th rows.

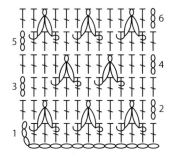

LCL

Sharp Chevron Stitch

Multiple of 14 sts.

(add 2 for base chain)

1st row: Skip 2ch (count as 1dc), 2dc into next ch, *1dc into each of next 3ch, [over next 3ch work dc3tog] twice, 1dc into each of next 3ch, [3dc into next st] twice; rep from * ending last rep with 3dc once only into last ch, turn.

2nd row: 3ch (count as 1dc), 2dc into first st, *1dc into each of next 3 sts, [over next 3 sts work dc3tog] twice, 1dc into each of next 3 sts, [3dc into next st] twice; rep from * ending last rep with 3dc once only into top of tch, turn.

Rep 2nd row.

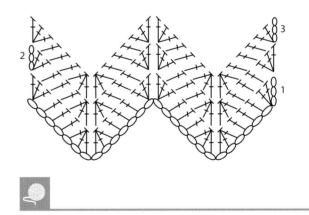

As there is generaly only one stitch on the hook, mistakes can easily be unraveled.

Open Shell and Picot Stitch

Multiple of 7 sts.

(add 1 for base chain)

1st row (right side): 1sc into 2nd ch from hook, *skip 2ch, work a Shell of [1dc, 1ch, 1dc, 1ch, 1dc] into next ch, skip 2ch, 1sc into next ch**, 3ch, 1sc into next ch; rep from * ending last rep at **, turn.

2nd row: 7ch (count as 1tr and 3ch), *work a Picot of [1sc, 3ch, 1sc] into center dc of next Shell, 3ch**, 1dc into next 3ch arch, 3ch; rep from * ending last rep at **, 1tr into last sc, skip tch, turn.

3rd row: 1ch, 1sc into first st, *skip next 3ch sp, Shell into center of next Picot, skip next 3ch sp**, Picot into next dc; rep from * ending last rep at **, 1sc into next ch of tch, turn.

Rep 2nd and 3rd rows.

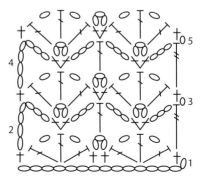

Broadway

Multiple of 8 sts + 2.

Special Abbreviations: Cr3R (Cross3Right) = skip 2sc, work 1tr into next sc, working behind last tr work 1dc into each of 2 skipped sc.

Cr3L (Cross3Left) = skip 1sc, work 1dc into each of next 2sc, working in front of last 2dc work 1tr into skipped sc.

1st row (wrong side): Work 1sc into 2nd ch from hook, 1sc into each ch to end, turn.

2nd row: 3ch (count as 1dc), skip first sc, *Cr3R, 1dc into next sc, Cr3L, 1dc into next sc; rep from * to end, turn.

3rd row: 1ch, work 1sc into each st to end placing last sc into 3rd of 3ch at beg of previous row, turn.

Rep 2nd and 3rd rows.

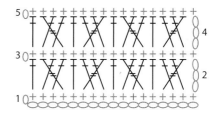

Cr3L

Cr3R

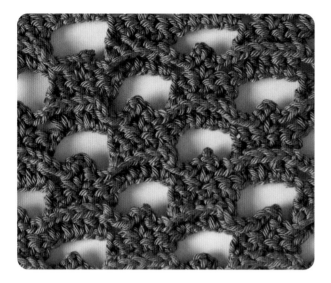

Picot Ridge Stitch

Multiple of 10 sts + 2.

(add 2 for base chain)

Special Abbreviation: dc/rf = Wrap the yarn around the hook, insert the hook from in front and from right to left around the stem of the appropriate stitch, and complete the stitch normally.

1st row (right side): Skip 3ch (count as 1dc), *1dc into each of next 5ch, 3ch, skip 2ch, [1sc, 4ch, 1sc] into next ch, 3ch, skip 2ch; rep from * ending 1dc into last ch, turn.

2nd row: 8ch (count as 1dc and 5ch), skip first st and next 3 arches, *1dc/rf around each of next 5 sts, 5ch, skip next 3 arches; rep from * ending 1dc/rf around each of last 5dcs, 1dc into top of tch, turn.

3rd row: 6ch, skip first 3 sts, *[1sc, 4ch, 1sc] into next st, 3ch, skip 2 sts, 1dc into each of next 5ch**, 3ch, skip 2 sts; rep from * ending last rep at **, 1dc into next ch of tch, turn.

4th row: 3ch (count as 1dc), skip first st, *1dc/rf around each of next 5 sts, 5ch**, skip next 3 arches; rep from * ending last rep at **, skip next 2 arches, 1dc into tch arch, turn.

5th row: 3ch (count as 1dc), skip first st, *1dc into each of next 5ch, 3ch, skip 2sts, [1sc, 4ch, 1sc] into next st, 3ch, skip 2 sts; rep from * ending 1dc into top of tch, turn.

Rep 2nd to 5th rows.

Single Crochet Cluster Stitch 1

Multiple of 2 sts + 1.

(add 1 for base chain)

1st row (wrong side): 1sc into 2nd ch from hook, *1ch, skip 1ch, 1sc into next ch; rep from * to end, turn.

2nd row: 1ch, 1sc into first st, 1ch, sc2tog inserting hook into each of next 2 ch sps, 1ch, *sc2tog inserting hook first into same ch sp as previous st then into next ch sp, 1ch; rep from * ending 1sc into last st, skip tch, turn.

3rd row: 1ch, 1sc into first st, *1ch, skip 1ch, 1sc into next st; rep from * to end, skip tch, turn.

Rep 2nd and 3rd rows.

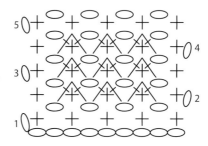

Single Crochet Cluster Stitch II

Multiple of 2 sts + 1.

(add 1 for base chain)

1st row: Skip 1ch, *sc2tog inserting hook into each of next 2ch, 1ch; rep from * ending 1sc into last ch, turn.

2nd row: 1ch, sc2tog inserting hook into first st then into next ch sp, 1ch, *sc2tog inserting hook first before and then after the vertical thread between the next 2 clusters, 1ch; rep from * ending 1sc into last sc, skip tch, turn.

Rep 2nd row.

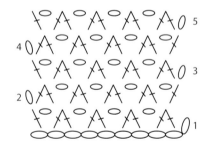

Single Crochet Cluster Stitch III

Multiple of 2 sts.

(add 1 for base chain)

1st row: Skip 2ch (count as 1hdc), *sc2tog inserting hook into each of next 2ch, 1ch; rep from * ending with 1hdc into last ch, turn.

2nd row: 2ch (count as 1hdc), skip 1 st, *sc2tog inserting hook into back loop only of next ch then into back loop only of next st, 1ch; rep from * ending with 1hdc into top of tch, turn.

Rep 2nd row.

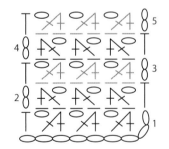

Single Crochet Cluster Stitch IV

Multiple of 2 sts + 1.

(add 1 for base chain)

Special Abbreviation: SC (Slip Cluster) = insert hook into ch or st as indicated, yo, draw loop through, insert hook again as indicated, yo, draw loop through st and through next loop on hook, yo, draw through last 2 loops on hook.

1st row: 1SC inserting hook into 2nd and then 3rd ch from hook, 1ch; *1SC inserting hook into each of next 2ch, 1ch; rep from * ending with 1sc into last ch, turn.

2nd row: 1ch, skip 1 st, *1SC inserting hook into front loop only of next ch then front loop only of next st, 1ch; rep from * ending 1sc into top of tch, turn.

Rep 2nd row.

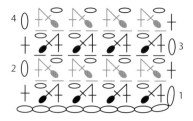

Close Chevron Stitch

Multiple of 11 sts +1.

(add 1 for base chain)

Work 4 rows each in colors A and B alternately throughout.

1st row (right side): 2sc into 2nd ch from hook, *1sc into each of next 4ch, skip 2ch, 1sc into each of next 4ch, 3sc into next ch; rep from * ending last rep with 2sc only into last ch, turn.

2nd row: 1ch, 2sc into first st, *1sc into each of next 4 sts, skip 2 sts, 1sc into each of next 4 sts, 3sc into next st; rep from * ending last rep with 2sc only into last st, skip tch, turn.

Rep 2nd row.

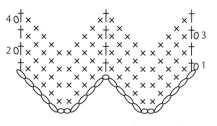

Ridged String Network

Multiple of 4 sts + 1.

(add 1 for base chain)

1st row (right side): 1sc into 2nd ch from hook, *3ch, skip 3ch, 1sc into next ch; rep from * to end, turn.

2nd row: 1ch, working into back loop only of each st work 1sc into first st, *3ch, skip 3ch, 1sc into next sc; rep from * to end, skip tch, turn.

Rep 2nd row.

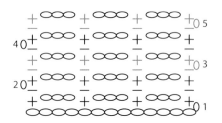

You can create a fabric with crochet from almost any length of continuous fiber—string, fabric, leather, even wire or plastic bags cut into strips!

Spatter Pattern

Multiple of 6 sts + 2.

1st row (right side): Work 1sc into 2nd ch from hook, *skip 2ch, 1dc into next ch, 2ch, into same ch as last dc work [1dc, 2ch, 1dc], skip 2ch, 1sc into next ch; rep from * to end, turn.

2nd row: 5ch (count as 1dc, 2ch), 1dc into first sc, skip 1dc, 1sc into next dc, *1dc into next sc, 2ch, into same st as last dc work [1dc, 2ch, 1dc], skip 1dc, 1sc into next dc; rep from * to last sc, into last sc work [1dc, 2ch, 1dc], turn.

3rd row: 1ch, 1sc into first dc, *1dc into next sc, 2ch, into same st as last dc work [1dc, 2ch, 1dc], skip 1dc, 1sc into next dc; rep from * to end placing last sc into 3rd of 5ch at beg of previous row, turn.

Rep 2nd and 3rd rows.

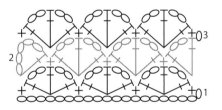

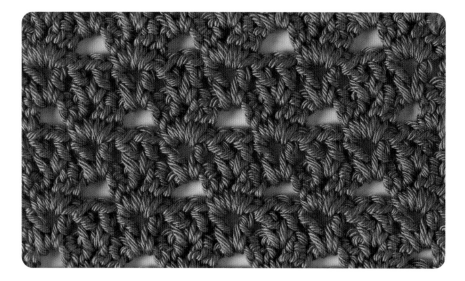

Basket Stitch

Multiple of 6 sts + 5.

(add 2 for base chain)

1st row (wrong side): Work a V st of [1dc, 1ch, 1dc] into 5th ch from hook, *skip 2ch, work V st into next ch; rep from * to last 2ch, skip 1ch, 1dc into last ch, turn.

2nd row: 3ch, skip 2 sts, work a Double V st of [2dc, 1ch, 2dc] into ch sp at center of V st, *1ch, skip next V st, work a Double V st into sp at center of next V st; rep from * leaving last loop of last dc of last Double V st on hook and working it together with 1dc into top of tch, turn.

3rd row: 3ch, work a V st into each sp to end finishing with 1dc into top of tch, turn.

4th row: 3ch, 1dc into first st, *1ch, skip next V st, work a Double V st into sp at center of next V st; rep from * until 1 V st remains, 1ch, skip V st, 2dc into top of tch, turn.

5th row: As 3rd row.

Rep 2nd to 5th rows.

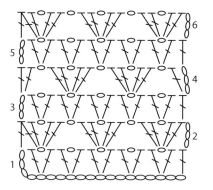

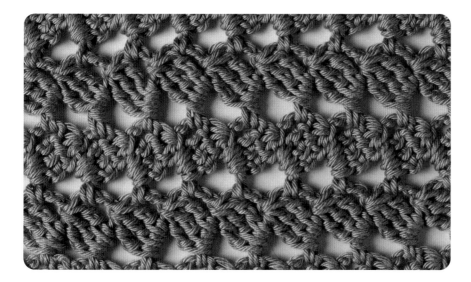

Connected Spiral

Multiple of 3 sts + 5.

Special Abbreviation: Cluster4 = work 3dc over stem of dc just worked but leaving last loop of each dc on hook, then work 4th dc as indicated leaving last loop as before (5 loops on hook), yo and through all 5 loops.

1st row (right side): Work 1dc into 6th ch from hook, *3ch, skip 2ch, work cluster4 placing 4th dc into next ch; rep from * to last 2ch, 3ch, work cluster4 placing 4th dc in last ch, turn.

2nd row: 3ch (count as 1dc), 1dc into next 3ch sp, *3ch, work cluster4 placing 4th dc into next 3ch sp; rep from * to end, placing final dc into top of ch at beg of previous row, turn.

Rep 2nd row.

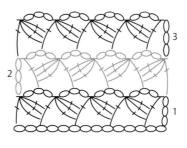

Cluster4

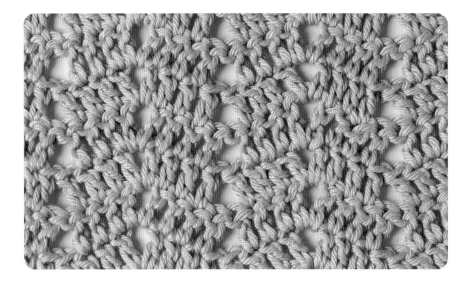

Peephole Chevron Stitch

Multiple of 10 sts.

(add 2 for base chain)

1st row: Skip 2ch (count as 1dc), 1dc into each of next 4ch, *skip 2ch, 1dc into each of next 4ch, 2ch, 1dc into each of next 4ch; rep from * to last 6ch, skip 2ch, 1dc into each of next 3ch, 2dc into last ch, turn.

2nd row: 3ch (count as 1dc), 1dc into first st, 1dc into each of next 3 sts, *skip 2 sts, 1dc into each of next 3 sts, [1dc, 2ch, 1dc] into 2ch sp, 1dc into each of next 3 sts; rep from * to last 6 sts, skip 2 sts, 1dc into each of next 3 sts, 2dc into top of tch, turn.

Rep 2nd row.

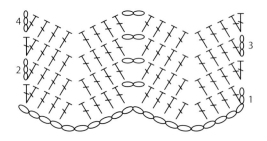

Search local hardware shops as well as traditional sewing stores for inspiration when looking for new yarns.

Double Picot String Network

Multiple of 6 sts + 5.

(add 1 for base chain)

1st row (wrong side): 1sc into 2nd ch from hook, 3ch, skip 4ch, work a picot of [1sc, 3ch, 1sc] into next ch, *3ch, skip 5ch, picot into next ch; rep from * to last 5ch, 3ch, skip 4ch, 1sc into last ch, turn.

2nd row: 1ch, 1sc into first st, *3ch, skip 3ch, 2 picots into next 3ch arch; rep from * ending 3ch, skip 3ch, 1sc into last sc, turn.

3rd row: 6ch (count as 1dc and 3ch), skip 3ch, *1sc into next picot arch, 3ch, 1sc into next picot arch, 3ch, skip 3ch; rep from * ending 1dc into last sc, skip tch, turn.

Rep 2nd and 3rd rows.

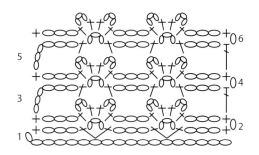

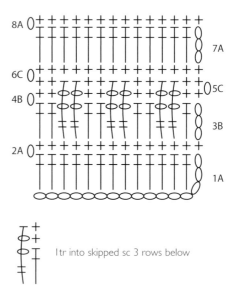

1tr into skipped sc 3 rows below

Tooth Pattern

Multiple of 4 sts + 4.

1st row (right side): Using A, work 1dc into 4th ch from hook, 1dc into each ch to end, turn.

2nd row: Using A, 1ch, work 1sc into each dc to end, working last sc into top of 3ch, turn.

3rd row: Using B, 3ch (count as 1dc), skip first sc, 1dc into next sc, *2ch, skip 2sc, 1dc into each of next 2sc; rep from * to end, turn.

4th row: Using B, 1ch, work 1sc into each of first 2dc, *2ch, 1sc into each of next 2dc; rep from * to end, working last sc into 3rd of 3ch at beg of previous row, turn.

5th row: Using C, 1ch, 1sc into each of first 2sc, *1tr into each of the 2 skipped sc 3 rows below, 1sc into each of next 2sc; rep from * to end, turn.

6th row: Using C, 1ch, 1sc into each sc and each tr to end, turn.

7th row: Using A, 3ch, skip first sc, 1dc into each sc to end, turn.

8th row: Using A, 1ch, 1sc into each dc to end, working last sc into 3rd of 3ch at beg of previous row, turn.
Rep 3rd to 8th rows.

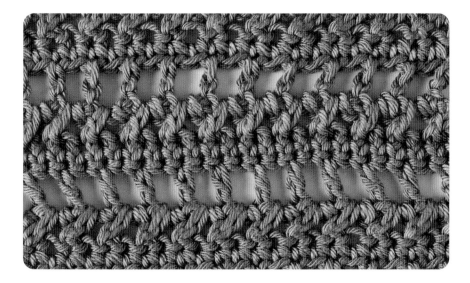

Zeros and Crosses Stitch

Multiple of 2 sts + 1.

(add 3 for base chain)

1st row (right side): 1dc into 6th ch from hook, *1ch, skip 1ch, 1dc into next ch; rep from * to end, turn.

2nd row: 3ch, skip next ch sp, work 2 crossed stitches as follows: 1dc forward into next ch sp, 1dc back into ch sp just skipped going behind forward dc so as not to catch it, *1dc forward into next unoccupied ch sp, 1dc back into previous ch sp going behind forward dc as before; rep from * to end when last forward dc occupies tch, 1dc into next ch, turn.

3rd row: 1ch, 1sc into first st, 1sc into next and each st to end, working last st into top of tch, turn.

4th row: 4ch (counts as 1dc and 1ch), skip 2 sts, 1dc into next st, *1ch, skip 1 st, 1dc into next st; rep from * ending last rep in tch, turn.

Rep 2nd to 4th rows.

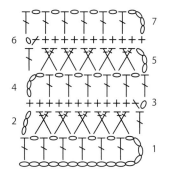

Half Double Crochet Cluster Stitch 1

Any number of sts.

(add 1 for base chain)

1st row: Skip 2ch (count as 1hdc), *hdc2tog all into next ch; rep from * to end, turn.

2nd row: 2ch (count as 1hdc), skip 1 st, hdc2tog all into next and each st, ending with hdc2tog into top of tch, turn.

Rep 2nd row.

Half Double Crochet Cluster Stitch II

Any number of sts.

(add 2 for base chain)

1st row: Skip 2ch (count as 1hdc), hdc2tog inserting hook into each of next 2ch, *hdc2tog inserting hook first into same ch as previous cluster then into next ch; rep from * until 1ch remains, 1hdc into last ch, turn.

2nd row: 2ch (count as 1hdc), hdc2tog inserting hook first into first st then into next st, *hdc2tog inserting hook first into same st as previous cluster then into next st; rep from * ending 1hdc into top of tch, turn.

Rep 2nd row.

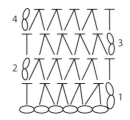

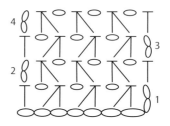

Half Double Crochet Cluster Stitch III

Multiple of 2 sts.

(add 1 for base chain)

1st row: Skip 2ch (count as 1hdc), *hdc2tog inserting hook into each of next 2ch, 1ch; rep from * ending 1hdc into last ch, turn.

2nd row: 2ch (count as 1hdc), skip 1 st, *hdc2tog inserting hook into next ch sp then into next st, 1ch; rep from * ending 1hdc into top of tch, turn.

Rep 2nd row.

Granule Stitch

Multiple of 4 sts + 1.

(add 1 for base chain)

Special Abbreviation: Psc (Picot single crochet) = insert hook, yo, draw loop through, [yo, draw through 1 loop] 3 times to make 3ch, yo, draw through both loops on hook.

Note: draw picot chain loops to the back (right side) of fabric.

1st row (right side): 1sc into 2nd ch from hook, 1sc into each ch to end, turn.

2nd row: 1ch, 1sc into first st, *1Psc into next st, 1sc into next st; rep from * to end, skip tch, turn.

3rd row: 1ch, 1sc into first and each st to end, skip tch, turn. **Hint:** Hold down the picot chains at the front and you will see the top 2 loops of the Psc where you are to insert the hook.

4th row: 1ch, 1sc into each of first 2 sts, *1Psc into next st, 1sc into next st; rep from * to last st, 1sc into last st, skip tch, turn.

5th row: As 3rd row.

Rep 2nd to 5th rows.

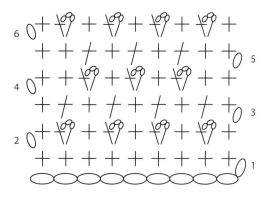

Crunchy Chevron Stitch

Multiple of 8 sts.

(add 1 for base chain)

Work 1 row each in colors A, B, C, D, and E throughout.

1st row: 1sc into 2nd ch from hook, 1sc into each of next 3ch, *hdc2tog all into each of next 4ch, 1sc into each of next 4ch; rep from * to last 4ch, hdc2tog all into each of last 4ch, turn.

2nd row: 1ch, then starting in first st, *1sc into each of next 4 sts, hdc2tog all into each of next 4sc; rep from * to end, skip tch, turn.

Rep 2nd row.

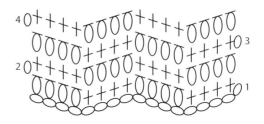

Experiment with different-sized hooks when using more unusual yarns, in order to achieve the desired fabric.

Forked Cluster Stitch

Any number of sts.

(add 2 for base chain)

Special Abbreviation: FC (Forked Cluster) = [yo, insert hook into ch or st as indicated, yo, draw loop through] twice (5 loops on hook), [yo, draw through 3 loops] twice.

1st row: Skip 2ch (count as 1dc), work 1FC inserting hook into each of next 2ch, *work 1FC inserting hook into same ch as previous FC then into next ch; rep from * until 1ch remains, 1dc into last ch, turn.

2nd row: 3ch (count as 1dc), 1FC inserting hook into each of first 2 sts, *1FC inserting hook into same st as previous FC then into next st; rep from * ending 1dc into top of tch, turn.

Rep 2nd row.

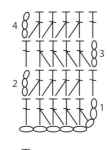

FC

Mirror Stitch

Multiple of 4 sts + 2.

1st row (right side): Using A, work 1sc into 2nd ch from hook, 1sc into next ch, *1ch, skip 1ch, 1sc into each of next 3ch; rep from * to end omitting 1sc at end of last rep, turn.

2nd row: Using A, 3ch (count as 1dc), skip first sc, work 1dc into next sc, *1ch, skip 1ch, 1dc into each of next 3sc; rep from * to end omitting 1dc at end of last rep, turn.

3rd row: Using B, 1ch, work 1sc into each of first 2dc, 1tr into first skipped starting ch, *1sc into next dc, 1ch, skip 1dc, 1sc into next dc, 1tr into next skipped starting ch; rep from * to last 2dc, 1sc into next dc, 1sc into 3rd of 3ch at beg of previous row, turn.

4th row: Using B, 3ch, skip first sc, work 1dc into each of next 3 sts, *1ch, skip 1ch, 1dc into each of next 3 sts; rep from * to last sc, 1dc into last sc, turn.

5th row: Using C, 1ch, work 1sc into each of first 2dc, *1ch, skip 1dc, 1sc into next dc, 1tr into next skipped dc 3 rows below, 1sc into next dc; rep from * to last 3dc, 1ch, skip 1dc, 1sc into next dc, 1sc into 3rd of 3ch at beg of previous row, turn.

6th row: Using C, 3ch, skip first sc, 1dc into next sc, *1ch, skip 1ch, 1dc into each of next 3 sts; rep from * to end omitting 1dc at end of last rep, turn.

7th row: Using A, 1ch, 1sc into each of first 2dc, 1tr into next skipped dc 3 rows below, *1sc into next dc, 1ch, skip 1dc, 1sc into next dc, 1tr into next skipped dc 3 rows below; rep from * to last 2dc, 1sc into each of last 2dc, turn.

8th row: As 4th row but using A instead of B.

Rep 5th to 8th rows continuing to work 2 rows each in colors B, C, and A as set.

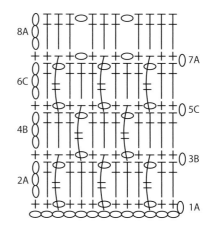

Work tr into skipped
st 3 rows below

Acrobatic Stitch

Multiple of 6 sts + 1.

(add 2 for base chain)

1st row (right side): 2dc into 3rd ch from hook, *4ch, skip 5ch, 5dc into next ch; rep from * working only 3dc at end of last rep, turn.

2nd row: 2ch (count as 1dc), skip first 3 sts, *work [3dc, 3ch, 3dc] into next 4ch arch**, skip next 5dc; rep from * ending last rep at **, skip 2dc, 1dc into top of tch, turn.

3rd row: 6ch (count as 1dtr and 1ch), *5dc into next 3ch arch**, 4ch; rep from * ending last rep at **, 1ch, 1dtr into top of tch, turn.

4th row: 5ch (count as 1tr and 1ch), 3dc into next 1ch sp, *skip 5dc, work [3dc, 3ch, 3dc] into next 4ch arch; rep from * ending skip 5dc, work [3dc, 1ch, 1tr] into tch, turn.

5th row: 3ch (count as 1dc), 2dc into next 1ch sp, *4ch, 5dc into next 3ch arch; rep from * ending 4ch, 3dc into tch, turn.

Rep 2nd to 5th rows.

Dots and Diamonds

Multiple of 4 sts + 3.

(add 1 for base chain)

Special Abbreviation: Psc (Picot single crochet) = insert hook, yo, draw loop through, [yo, draw through 1 loop] 3 times, yo, draw through both loops on hook. Draw picot ch loops to front (right side) of fabric.

Tr/rf2tog = *yo twice, insert hook as indicated, yo, draw loop through, (yo, draw through 2 loops) twice*.

Base row (right side): 1sc into 2nd ch from hook, 1sc into each of next 2ch, *Psc into next ch, 1sc into each of next 3ch; rep from * to end, turn.

1st row: 3ch (count as 1dc), skip first st, 1dc into each st to end, skip tch, turn.

2nd row: 1ch, 1sc into first st, *Psc into next st, 1sc into next st**, tr/rf2tog over next st inserting hook around 2nd sc in second-to-last row for first leg and around following 4th sc for 2nd leg (skipping 3 sts between), 1sc into next st; rep from * ending last rep at ** in top of tch, turn.

3rd row: As 1st row.

4th row: 1ch, 1sc into first st, 1tr/rf over next st inserting hook around top of first raised cluster 2 rows below, *1sc into next st, Psc into next st, 1sc into next st**, tr/rf2tog over next st inserting hook around same cluster as last raised st for first leg and around top of next raised cluster for 2nd leg; rep from * ending last rep at ** when 2 sts remain, 1tr/rf over next st inserting hook around top of same cluster as last raised st, 1sc into top of tch, turn.

5th row: As 1st row.

6th row: As 2nd row, except to make new raised clusters insert hook around previous raised clusters instead of scs.

Rep 3rd to 6th rows.

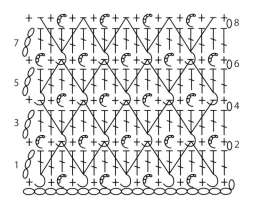

ℓ   Psc

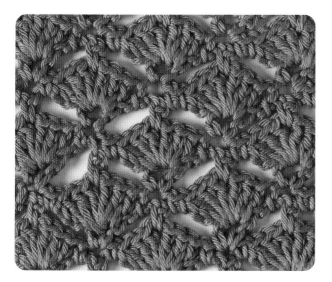

Fantail Stitch

Multiple of 10 sts + 1.

(add 1 for base chain)

1st row (right side): 1sc into 2nd ch from hook, 1sc into next ch, *skip 3ch, work a Fan of [3dc, 1ch, 3dc] into next ch, skip 3ch, 1sc into next ch**, 1ch, skip 1ch, 1sc into next ch; rep from * ending last rep at **, 1sc into last ch, turn.

2nd row: 2ch (count as 1hdc), 1hdc into first st, *3ch, 1sc into ch sp at center of next Fan, 3ch**, work a V st of [1hdc, 1ch, 1hdc] into next sp; rep from * ending last rep at **, 2hdc into last sc, skip tch, turn.

3rd row: 3ch, 3dc into first st, *1sc into next 3ch arch, 1ch, 1sc into next arch**, work a Fan into sp at center of next V st; rep from * ending last rep at **, 4dc into top of tch, turn.

4th row: 1ch, 1sc into first st, *3ch, V st into next sp, 3ch, 1sc into sp at center of next Fan; rep from * ending last rep into top of tch, turn.

5th row: 1ch, 1sc into first st, *1sc into next arch, Fan into sp at center of next V st, 1sc into next arch**, 1ch; rep from * ending last rep at **, 1sc into last sc, skip tch, turn.

Rep 2nd to 5th rows.

Mat Stitch

Multiple of 6 sts + 2.

1st row (right side): Work 1sc into 2nd ch from hook, *skip 2ch, 1dc into next ch, 1ch, into same ch as last dc work [1dc, 1ch, 1dc], skip 2ch, 1sc into next ch; rep from * to end, turn.

2nd row: 4ch (count as 1dc, 1ch), 1dc into first sc, skip 1dc, 1sc into next dc, *1dc into next sc, 1ch, into same st as last dc work [1dc, 1ch, 1dc], skip 1dc, 1sc into next dc; rep from * to last sc, into last sc work [1dc, 1ch, 1dc], turn.

3rd row: 1ch, 1sc into first dc, *1dc into next sc, 1ch, into same st as last dc work [1dc, 1ch, 1dc], skip 1dc, 1sc into next dc; rep from * to end placing last sc into 3rd of 4ch at beg of previous row, turn.

Rep 2nd and 3rd rows.

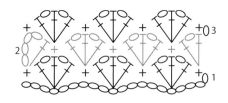

Always read the pattern through before starting!

Simple Chevron Stitch

Multiple of 10 sts + 1.

(add 2 for base chain)

1st row: Skip 2ch (count as 1dc), 1dc into next ch, *1dc into each of next 3ch, over next 3ch work dc3tog, 1dc into each of next 3ch, 3dc into next ch; rep from * ending last rep with 2dc into last ch, turn.

2nd row: 3ch (count as 1dc), 1dc into first st, *1dc into each of next 3dc, over next 3 sts work dc3tog, 1dc into each of next 3dc, 3dc into next dc; rep from * ending last rep with 2dc into top of tch, turn.

Rep 2nd row.

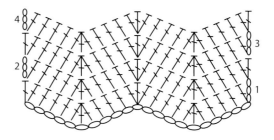

Cabbage Patch

Multiple of 4 sts + 7.

Special Abbreviation: Cross2dc = skip 3dc, work 1dc into next dc, 2ch, working behind last dc work 1dc into the first of the skipped dc.

1st row (right side): Work 4dc into 5th ch from hook, *skip 3ch, 4dc into next ch; rep from * to last 2ch, 1dc into last ch, turn.

2nd row: 3ch (count as 1dc), skip first dc, *cross2dc; rep from * to end, 1dc into top of 3ch at beg of previous row, turn.

3rd row: 3ch, work 4dc into each 2ch sp to end, 1dc into 3rd of 3ch at beg of previous row, turn.

Rep 2nd and 3rd rows.

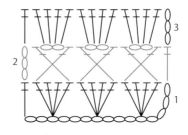

Cross2dc

Relief Arch Stitch

Multiple of 8 sts + 1.

(add 1 for base chain)

1st row (wrong side): 1sc into 2nd ch from hook, 1sc into each of next 2ch, *7ch, skip 3ch, 1sc into each of next 5ch; rep from * to last 6ch, 7ch, skip 3ch, 1sc into each of last 3ch, turn.

2nd row: 3ch (count as 1dc), skip 1 st, 1dc into each of next 2 sts, *going behind 7ch loop work 1tr into each of next 3 base ch**, 1dc into each of next 5sc; rep from * ending last rep at ** when 3 sts remain, 1dc into each of last 3 sts, skip tch, turn.

3rd row: 1ch, 1sc into first st, *7ch, skip 3 sts, 1sc into next st at same time catching in center of 7ch loop of second-to-last row, 7ch, skip 3 sts, 1sc into next st; rep from * to end, turn.

4th row: 3ch (count as 1dc), skip 1 st, *going behind 7ch loop of last row work 1tr into each of next 3 sts of second-to-last row, 1dc into next sc; rep from * to end, skip tch, turn.

5th row: 1ch, 1sc into each of first 2 sts, *1sc into next st at same time catching in center of 7ch loop of second-to-last row, 7ch, skip 3 sts, 1sc into next st at same time catching in center of 7ch loop of second-to-last row**, 1sc into each of next 3 sts; rep from * ending last rep at ** when 2 sts remain, 1sc into each of last 2 sts, turn.

6th row: As 2nd row working trs into second-to-last row.

Rep 3rd to 6th rows.

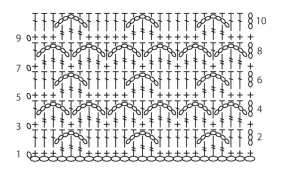

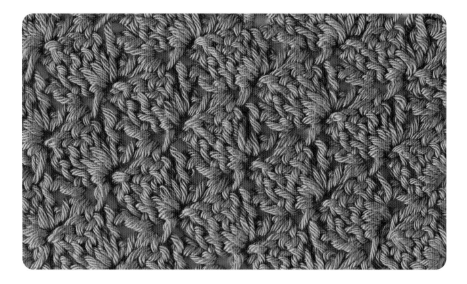

Flying Shell Stitch

Multiple of 4 sts + 1.

(add 1 for base chain)

1st row (right side): Work a Flying Shell (called FS) of [1sc, 3ch, 3dc] into 2nd ch from hook, *skip 3ch, 1FS into next ch; rep from * to last 4ch, skip 3ch, 1sc into last ch, turn.

2nd row: 3ch, 1dc into first st, *skip 3 sts, 1sc into top of 3ch**, work a V st of [1dc, 1ch, 1dc] into next sc; rep from * ending last rep at **, 2dc into last sc, skip tch, turn.

3rd row: 3ch, 3dc into first st, skip next st, *1FS into next sc, skip next V st; rep from * ending 1sc into last sc, 3ch, dc2tog over last dc and top of tch, turn.

4th row: 1ch, *V st into next sc, skip 3 sts, 1sc into top of 3ch; rep from * to end, turn.

5th row: 1ch, FS into first st, *skip next V st, FS into next sc; rep from * ending skip last V st, 1sc into tch, turn.

Rep 2nd to 5th rows.

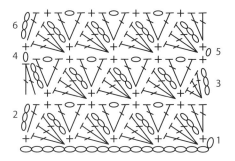

Corded Ridge Stitch

Any number of sts.

(add 2 for base chain)

Note: Work all rows with right side facing—for example, work even-numbered rows from left to right.

1st row (right side): Skip 3ch (count as 1dc), 1dc into next and each ch to end. Do not turn.

2nd row: 1ch, 1sc into front loop only of last dc made, *1sc into front loop only of next dc to right; rep from * ending sl st into top of tch at beginning of row. Do not turn.

3rd row: 3ch (count as 1dc), skip 1 st, 1dc into back loop only of next and each st of second-to-last row to end. Do not turn.

Rep 2nd and 3rd rows.

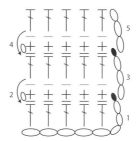

Wedge Stitch I

Multiple of 6 sts + 1.

(add 1 for base chain)

Special Abbreviation: WP (Wedge Picot) = work 6ch, 1sc into 2nd ch from hook, 1hdc into next ch, 1dc into next ch, 1tr into next ch, 1dtr into next ch.

1st row (wrong side): 1sc into 2nd ch from hook, *1WP, skip 5ch, 1sc into next ch; rep from * to end, turn.

2nd row: 5ch (count as 1dtr), *1sc into top of WP, over next 5ch at underside of WP work 1sc into next ch, 1hdc into next ch, 1dc into next ch, 1tr into next ch, 1dtr into next ch, skip next sc; rep from * omitting 1dtr at end of last rep when 2 sts remain, **[yo] 3 times, insert hook into last ch at underside of WP, yo, draw loop through, [yo, draw through 2 loops] 3 times, rep from ** into next sc,

yo, draw through all 3 loops on hook, skip tch, turn.

3rd row: 1ch, 1sc into first st, *1WP, skip next 5 sts, 1sc into next st; rep from * ending last rep with 1sc into top of tch, turn.

Rep 2nd and 3rd rows.

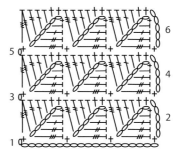

Wedge Stitch II

Work as Wedge Stitch I (page 88).

Make base chain and work first row in color A.

Thereafter, work 2 rows each in color B and color A.

Don't be put off if you're new to crochet. Hold the hook like a pencil, or between your thumb and forefinger like a knife: whatever feels comfortable is okay.

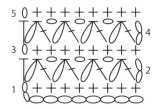

Mixed Cluster Stitch

Multiple of 2 sts + 1.

(add 1 for base chain)

Special Abbreviation: MC (Mixed Cluster) = yo, insert hook into first st as indicated, yo, draw loop through, yo, draw through 2 loops, skip 1 st, [yo, insert hook into next st, yo, draw loop through] twice all into same st, (6 loops on hook), yo, draw through all loops on hook.

1st row (wrong side): Skip 2ch (count as 1sc), 1sc into next and each ch to end, turn.

2nd row: 2ch (count as 1hdc), 1MC inserting hook into first then 3rd st, *1ch, 1MC inserting hook first into same st as previous MC; rep from * ending last rep in top of tch, 1hdc into same place, turn.

3rd row: 1ch, skip 1 st, 1sc into next and each st to end, working last st into top of tch, turn.

Rep 2nd and 3rd rows.

MC

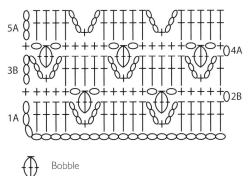

◈ Bobble

Crown Pattern

Multiple of 8 sts + 7.

Special Abbreviation: Bobble = work 3dc into next sc until last loop of each dc remains on hook, yo and through all 4 loops.

Note: Count each sc, ch sp and bobble as 1 st throughout.

1st row (wrong side): Using A, work 1dc into 4th ch from hook, 1dc into each of next 3ch, *3ch, skip 1ch, 1sc into next ch, 3ch, skip 1ch, 1dc into each of next 5ch; rep from * to end, turn.

2nd row: Using B, 1ch, work 1sc into each of first 5dc, *1ch, 1 bobble into next sc, 1ch, 1sc into each of next 5dc; rep from * to end placing last sc into top of 3ch, turn.

3rd row: Using B, 6ch (count as 1dc, 3ch), skip first 2sc, 1sc into next sc, 3ch, *skip 1sc, 1dc into each of next 5 sts (see note above), 3ch, skip 1sc, 1sc into next sc, 3ch; rep from * to last 2sc, skip 1sc, 1dc into last sc, turn.

4th row: Using A, 1ch, work 1sc into first dc, 1ch, 1 bobble into next sc, 1ch, *1sc into each of next 5dc, 1ch, 1 bobble into next sc, 1ch; rep from * to last dc, 1sc into 3rd of 6ch at beg of previous row, turn.

5th row: Using A, 3ch (count as 1dc), skip first sc, 1dc into each of next 4 sts, *3ch, skip 1sc, 1sc into next sc, 3ch, skip 1sc, 1dc into each of next 5 sts; rep from * to end, turn. Rep 2nd to 5th rows.

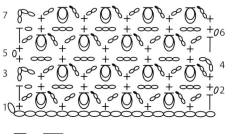

$\overline{O}$ = (tr7tog symbol) tr7tog

Pebble Lace Stitch

Multiple of 4 sts + 3.

(add 1 for base chain)

Note: Close tr7tog clusters with 1ch drawn tightly, (this does not count as part of following ch loop).

Clusters always occur on wrong-side rows. Be sure to push them all out to the back (right side) of the fabric as you complete them.

1st row (wrong side): 1sc into 2nd ch from hook, *2ch, skip 1ch, work tr7tog into next ch, 2ch, skip 1ch, 1sc into next ch; rep from * to last 2ch, 2ch, skip 1ch, 1hdc into last ch, turn.

2nd row: 1ch, 1sc into first st, *3ch, 1sc into next cluster; rep from * ending 1ch, 1hdc into last sc, skip tch, turn.

3rd row: 4ch, skip first hdc and ch, 1sc into next sc, *2ch, tr7tog into 2nd of next 3ch, 2ch, 1sc into next sc; rep from * to end, skip tch, turn.

4th row: 3ch, skip first st and 2ch, 1sc into next cluster; *3ch, 1sc into next cluster; rep from * ending 3ch, 1sc into last 4ch arch, turn.

5th row: 1ch, 1sc into first st, *2ch, tr7tog into 2nd of next 3ch, 2ch, 1sc into next sc; rep from * ending 2ch, skip 1ch, 1hdc into next ch of tch, turn.

Rep 2nd to 5th rows.

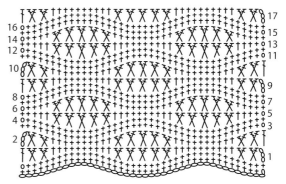

Textured Wave Stitch

Multiple of 20 sts.

(add 1 for base chain)

Special Abbreviation: 2Cdc (2 crossed double crochets)
= skip next st, 1dc into next st, 1dc into skipped st
working over previous dc.

Work 2 rows each in colors A and B alternately
throughout.

1st base row (right side): Skip 2ch (count as 1sc), 1sc
into next and each ch to end, turn.

2nd base row: 1ch (counts as 1sc), skip 1 st, 1sc into next
and each st to end working last st into tch, turn.

Commence Pattern

1st row: 3ch (count as 1dc), skip 1 st, over next 4 sts
work [2Cdc] twice, *1sc into each of next 10 sts, over
next 10 sts work [2Cdc] 5 times; rep from * to last 15 sts,
1sc into each of next 10 sts, over next 4 sts work [2Cdc]
twice, 1dc into tch, turn.

2nd row: As 1st row.

3rd and 4th rows: As 2nd base row.

5th row: 1ch (counts as 1sc), skip 1 st, 1sc into each of
next 4 sts, *over next 10 sts work [2Cdc] 5 times, 1sc into
each of next 10 sts; rep from * to last 15 sts, over next 10
sts work [2Cdc] 5 times, 1sc into each of last 5 sts
working last st into tch, turn.

6th row: As 5th row.

7th and 8th rows: As 2nd base row.

Rep these 8 rows.

Double Crochet Cluster Stitch I

Multiple of 2 sts.

(add 2 for base chain)

Special Abbreviation: DcC (Double Crochet Cluster) = *yo, insert hook into ch or st as indicated, yo, draw loop through, yo, draw through 2 loops*, skip 1 ch or st, rep from * to * into next st, yo, draw through all 3 loops on hook.

1st row: Skip 2ch (count as 1dc), work 1DcC inserting hook first into 3rd ch, 1ch, *work 1DcC inserting hook first into same ch as previous DcC, 1ch; rep from * ending 1dc into last ch, turn.

2nd row: 3ch (counts as 1dc), 1DcC inserting hook first into first st, 1ch, *1DcC inserting hook first into same st as previous DcC, 1ch; rep from * ending 1dc into top of tch, turn.

Rep 2nd row.

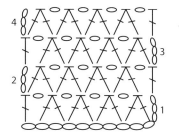

Double Crochet Cluster Stitch II

Multiple of 2 sts.

(add 2 for base chain)

Special Abbreviation: DcC (Double Crochet Cluster) = work as under Double Crochet Cluster Stitch I.

1st row (right side): Skip 2ch (count as 1dc), work 1DcC inserting hook into 3rd ch then 5th ch, 1ch, *work 1DcC inserting hook first into same ch as previous DcC, 1ch; rep from * ending 1dc into last ch, turn.

2nd row: 1ch, skip 1st, *1sc into next ch sp, 1ch, skip 1 st; rep from * ending 1sc into top of tch, turn.

3rd row: 3ch (count as 1dc), 1DcC inserting hook first into first st, 1ch, *1DcC inserting hook first into same st as previous DcC, 1ch; rep from * ending 1dc into top of tch, turn.

Rep 2nd and 3rd rows.

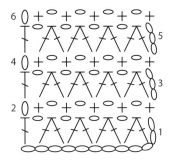

Double Crochet Cluster Stitch III

Any number of sts.

(add 2 for base chain)

1st row: Skip 3ch (count as 1dc), work dc2tog into next and each ch until 1ch remains, 1dc into last ch, turn.

2nd row: 3ch (count as 1dc), dc2tog between first dc and next cluster, *dc2tog between next 2 clusters; rep from * ending 1dc into top of tch, turn.

Rep 2nd row.

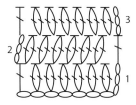

Thistle Pattern

Multiple of 10 sts + 1.

(add 1 for base chain)

Special Abbreviation: Catch Loop = Catch 10ch loop of Thistle by inserting hook under ch at tip of loop at the same time as under the next st.

Base row (wrong side): Skip 2ch (count as 1sc), 1sc into each of next 4ch, *into next st work a Thistle of 1sc, [10ch, 1sc] 3 times**, 1sc into each of next 9ch; rep from * ending last rep at **, 1sc into each of last 5sc, turn.

Commence Pattern

Note: Hold loops of Thistle down at front of work on right-side rows.

1st row: 1ch (count as 1sc), skip 1sc, 1sc into each of next 4sc, *skip 1sc of Thistle, work sc2tog over next 2sc, skip last sc of Thistle**, work 1sc into each of next 9 sts; rep from * ending last rep at **, 1sc into each of next 4sc, 1sc into tch, turn.

2nd, 4th, 8th, and 10th rows: 1ch, skip 1 st, 1sc into each st to end, turn.

3rd row: 1ch, skip 1 st, 1sc into next sc, *catch first loop of Thistle in next sc, 1sc into each of next 5sc, skip center loop of Thistle, catch 3rd loop in next st**, 1sc into each of next 3sc; rep from * ending last rep at **, 1sc into each of last 2 sts, turn.

5th row: 1ch, skip 1 st, 1sc into each of next 4sc, *work 6dc into next sc and at the same time catch center loop**, 1sc into each of next 9sc; rep from * ending last rep at **, 1sc into each of last 5 sts, turn.

6th row: 1ch, skip 1 st, 1sc into each of first 4sc, *1ch, skip 6dc, 1sc into each of next 4sc**, work a Thistle into next sc, 1sc into each of next 4sc; rep from * ending last rep at **, 1sc into last st, turn.

7th row: 1ch, skip 1 st, 1sc into each of next 9 sts, *work sc2tog over center 2 of next 4sc, skip 1sc, 1sc into each of next 9 sts; rep from * to last st, 1sc into last st, turn.

9th row: 1ch, skip 1 st, 1sc into each of next 6sc, *catch first loop into next sc, 1sc into each of next 5sc, catch 3rd loop into next sc**, 1sc into each of next 3sc; rep from * ending last rep at **, 1sc into each st to end, turn.

11th row: 1ch, skip 1 st, 1sc into each of next 9 sts, *work 6dc into next sc and catch center loop at the same time, 1sc into each of next 9sc; rep from * to last st, 1sc in last st, turn.

12th row: 1ch, skip 1st, 1sc into each of next 4sc, *work a

Thistle into next sc, 1sc into each of next 4sc**, 1ch, skip 6dc, 1sc into each of next 4sc; rep from * ending last rep at **, 1sc into last st, turn.

Rep these 12 rows.

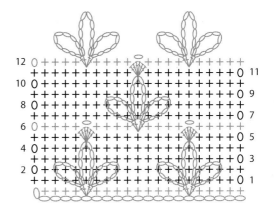

To give a firm edge to your crochet when you reach the last vertical bar when drawing up loops, insert the hook through the last vertical bar and the stitch directly behind it and draw up a loop.

Floret Stitch I

Multiple of 2 sts + 1.

(add 2 for base chain)

1st row (right side): Skip 3ch (count as 1dc), 1dc into next and each ch to end, turn.

2nd row: 1ch, skip 1 st, *1dc into next st, sl st into next st; rep from * ending last rep into top of tch, turn.

3rd row: 3ch (count as 1dc), skip 1 st, *1dc into next dc, 1dc into next sl st; rep from * ending last rep into tch, turn.

Rep 2nd and 3rd rows.

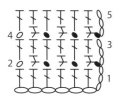

Floret Stitch II

Work as Floret Stitch I (this page).

Work 1 row each in colors A and B alternately throughout.

Floret Stitch III

Work as Floret Stitch I (page 98).

Work 1 row each in colors A, B, and C throughout.

When you come to the end of the row or round, you need to finish or end off the yarn securely. Cut the yarn leaving at least six inches (you may need to leave more for sewing seams or if the pattern instructs otherwise). Yarn over and draw through the last loop on your hook to finish off. Pull the end of the yarn, that was drawn through to secure.

Crunch Stitch

Multiple of 2 sts.

(add 1 for base chain)

1st row: Skip 2ch (count as 1hdc), *sl st into next ch, 1hdc into next ch; rep from * ending sl st into last ch, turn.

2nd row: 2ch (count as 1hdc), skip 1 st, *sl st into next hdc, 1hdc into next sl st; rep from * ending sl st into top of tch, turn.

Rep 2nd row.

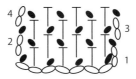

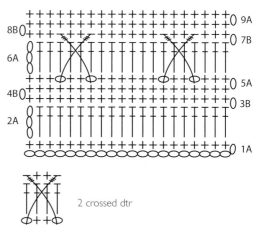

2 crossed dtr

Slot Stitch

Multiple of 10 sts + 1.

Using A make required number of chains.

1st row (right side): Using A, work 1sc into 2nd ch from hook, 1sc into each ch to end, turn.

2nd row: Using A, 3ch (count as 1dc), skip first sc, work 1dc into each sc to end, turn.

3rd row: Using B, 1ch, work 1sc into each dc to end placing last sc into 3rd of 3ch at beg of previous row, turn.

4th row: Using B, 1ch, work 1sc into each sc to end, turn.

5th row: Using A, 1ch, work 1sc into each of first 3sc, *1ch, skip 1sc, 1sc into each of next 2sc, 1ch, skip 1sc, 1sc into each of next 6sc; rep from * to end omitting 3sc at end of last rep, turn.

On 6th row work dc into ch not ch space.

6th row: Using A, 3ch (count as 1dc), skip first sc, 1dc into each sc and into each ch to end, turn.

7th row: Using B, 1ch, 1sc into each of first 3dc, *work 1dtr into 2nd skipped sc 3 rows below, skip 1dc, 1sc into each of next 2dc, 1dtr into first skipped sc 3 rows below (thus crossing 2dtr), skip 1dc, 1sc into each of next 6dc; rep from * to end omitting 3sc at end of last rep and placing last sc into 3rd of 3ch at beg of previous row, turn.

8th row: Using B, 1ch, work 1sc into each st to end, turn.

9th row: Using A, 1ch, work 1sc into each sc to end, turn.

Rep 2nd to 9th rows.

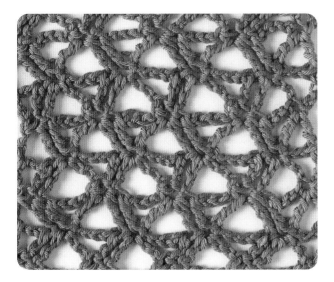

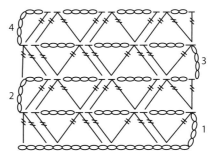

Doubled Lattice Stitch

Multiple of 6 sts + 2.

(add 3 for base chain)

1st row (right side): Skip 6ch, 1tr into next ch (counts as edge cluster), 4ch, 1tr into same ch as tr just made, *tr2tog inserting hook into next ch for first leg and then into following 5th ch for 2nd leg (skipping 4ch between), 4ch, 1tr into same ch as 2nd leg of cluster just made; rep from * to last 4ch, tr2tog inserting hook into next ch for first leg and into last ch for 2nd leg (skipping 2ch between), turn.

2nd row: 6ch (count as 1tr and 2ch), 1tr into first st, *tr2tog inserting hook into next tr for first leg and then into next cluster for 2nd leg**, 4ch, 1tr into same place as 2nd leg of cluster just made; rep from * ending last rep at ** when 2nd leg is in edge cluster, 2ch, 1tr into same place, turn.

3rd row: 4ch, skip 2ch, 1tr into next cluster (counts as edge cluster), *4ch, 1tr into same place as tr just made**, tr2tog inserting hook into next tr for first leg and then into next cluster for 2nd leg; rep from * ending last rep at **, tr2tog inserting hook into next tr for first leg and then into following 3rd ch for 2nd leg, turn.

Rep 2nd and 3rd rows.

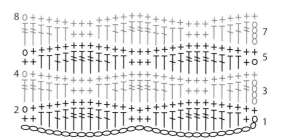

Long Wave Stitch

Multiple of 14 sts + 1.

(add 1 for base chain)

Special Abbreviations: Gr (Group) (worked over 14 sts)
= 1sc into next st, [1hdc into next st] twice, [1dc into next st] twice, [1tr into next st] 3 times, [1dc into next st] twice, [1hdc into next st] twice, [1sc into next st] twice.

Rev Gr (Reverse Group) (worked over 14 sts) = 1tr into next st, [1dc into next st] twice, [1hdc into next st] twice, [1sc into next st] 3 times, [1hdc into next st] twice, [1dc into next st] twice, [1tr into next st] twice.

Work 2 rows each in colors A and B alternately throughout.

1st row (right side): Skip 2ch (count as 1sc), *1Gr over next 14ch; rep from * to end, turn.

2nd row: 1ch (counts as 1sc), skip first st, 1sc into next and each st to end working last st into top of tch, turn.

3rd row: 4ch (count as 1tr), skip first st, *1 Rev Gr over next 14 sts; rep from * ending last rep in tch, turn.

4th row: As 2nd row.

5th row: 1ch (counts as 1sc), skip first st, *1Gr over next 14 sts; rep from * ending last rep in tch, turn.

6th row: As 2nd row.

Rep 3rd to 6th rows.

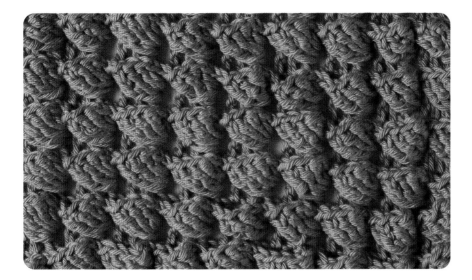

Embossed Pockets

Multiple of 3 sts + 1.

(add 2 for base chain)

Special Abbreviation: PGr (Pocket Group) = work [1sc, 1hdc, 3dc] around stem of indicated st.

1st row (wrong side): Skip 3ch (count as 1dc), 1dc into each ch to end, turn.

2nd row: 1PGr around first st, skip 2 sts, sl st into top of next st, *1PGr around same st as sl st, skip 2 sts, sl st into top of next st; rep from * to end, turn.

3rd row: 3ch (count as 1dc), skip 1 st, 1dc into each st to end, turn.

Rep 2nd and 3rd rows.

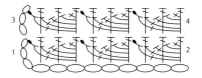

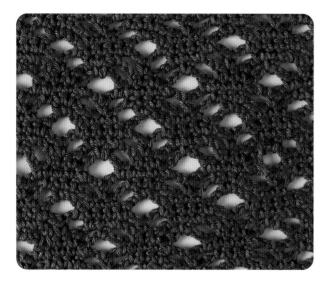

Triple Curve Stitch

Multiple of 8 sts + 2.

1st row (wrong side): Work 1sc into 2nd ch from hook, 1sc into next ch to end, turn.

2nd row: 1ch, 1sc into each of first 3sc, *5ch, skip 3sc, 1sc into each of next 5sc; rep from * to end omitting 2sc at end of last rep, turn.

3rd row: 1ch, 1sc into each of first 2sc, *3ch, 1sc into next 5ch arch, 3ch, skip 1sc, 1sc into each of next 3sc; rep from * to end omitting 1sc at end of last rep, turn.

4th row: 1ch, 1sc into first sc, *3ch, 1sc into next 3ch arch, 1sc into next sc, 1sc into next 3ch arch, 3ch, skip 1sc, 1sc into next sc; rep from * to end, turn.

5th row: 5ch (count as 1dc, 2ch), 1sc into next 3ch arch, 1sc into each of next 3sc, 1sc into next 3ch arch, *5ch, 1sc into next 3ch arch, 1sc into each of next 3sc, 1sc into next 3ch arch; rep from * to last sc, 2ch, 1dc into last sc, turn.

6th row: 1ch, 1sc into first dc, 3ch, skip 1sc, 1sc into each of next 3sc, *3ch, 1sc into next 5ch arch, 3ch, skip 1sc, 1sc into each of next 3sc; rep from * to last 2ch arch, 3ch, 1sc into 3rd of 5ch at beg of previous row, turn.

7th row: 1ch, 1sc into first sc, 1sc into first 3ch arch, 3ch, skip 1sc, 1sc into next sc, *3ch, 1sc into next 3ch arch, 1sc into next sc, 1sc into next 3ch arch, 3ch, skip 1sc, 1sc into next sc; rep from * to last 3ch arch, 3ch, 1sc into 3ch arch, 1sc into last sc, turn.

8th row: 1ch, 1sc into each of first 2sc, *1sc into next 3ch arch, 5ch, 1sc into next 3ch arch, 1sc into each of next 3sc; rep from * to end omitting 1sc at end of last rep, turn.

Rep 3rd to 8th rows.

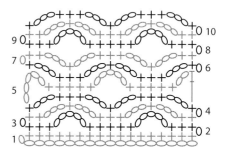

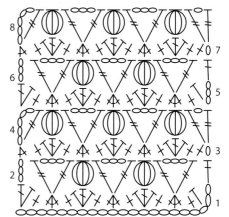

Crown Puff Lattice

Multiple of 6 sts + 1.

(add 2 for base chain)

1st row (right side): 1hdc into 3rd ch from hook, *1sc into next ch, sc3tog over next 3ch, 1sc into next ch, [1hdc, 1dc, 1hdc] into next ch; rep from * omitting 1hdc at end of last rep, turn.

2nd row: 3ch (count as 1dc), skip first 3 sts, *[1tr, 3ch, 1tr] into next sc cluster, skip 2 sts**, work hdc5tog into next dc; rep from * ending last rep at **, 1dc into top of tch, turn.

3rd row: 1ch, skip 1 st, 1sc into next tr (all counts as sc cluster), *[1sc, 1hdc, 1dc, 1hdc, 1sc] into next 3ch arch**, sc3tog over next 3 sts; rep from * ending last rep at **, sc2tog over last st and top of tch, turn.

4th row: 5ch (count as 1tr and 1ch), 1tr into first st, *skip 2 sts, hdc5tog into next dc, skip 2 sts**, [1tr, 3ch, 1tr] into next sc cluster; rep from * ending last rep at **, [1tr, 1ch, 1tr] into top of tch, turn.

5th row: 3ch (count as 1dc), 1hdc into first st, 1sc into next ch sp, *sc3tog over next 3 sts**, [1sc, 1hdc, 1dc, 1hdc, 1sc] into next 3ch arch; rep from * ending last rep at **, 1sc into next ch of tch, [1hdc, 1dc] into next ch, turn.

Rep 2nd to 5th rows.

Griddle Stitch

Multiple of 2 sts.

(add 2 for base chain)

1st row: Skip 3ch (count as 1dc), *1sc into next ch, 1dc into next ch; rep from * ending 1sc into last ch, turn.

2nd row: 3ch (count as 1dc), skip 1 st, *1sc into next dc, 1dc into next sc; rep from * ending 1sc into top of tch, turn.

Rep 2nd row.

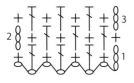

Crumpled Griddle Stitch

Multiple of 2 sts + 1.

(add 2 for base chain)

1st row: Skip 3ch (count as 1dc), *1sc into next ch, 1dc into next ch; rep from * to end, turn.

2nd row: 3ch (count as 1dc), skip 1 st, *1sc into next sc, 1dc into next dc; rep from * ending last rep into top of tch, turn.

Rep 2nd row.

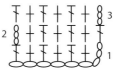

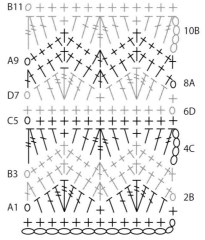

Wave and Chevron Stitch

Multiple of 6 sts + 1.

(add 1 for base chain)

Work 2 rows each in colors A, B, C, and D throughout.

Base row (right side): Skip 2ch (count as 1sc), 1sc into next and each ch to end, turn.

Commence Pattern

1st row: 1ch (counts as 1sc), skip 1 st, *1hdc into next st, 1dc into next st, 3tr into next st, 1dc into next st, 1hdc into next st, 1sc into next st; rep from * to end, turn.

2nd row: 1ch, skip 1 st, 1sc into next st (counts as sc2tog), 1sc into each of next 2 sts, *3sc into next st, 1sc into each of next 2 sts, over next 3 sts work sc3tog, 1sc into each of next 2 sts; rep from * to last 5 sts, 3sc into next st, 1sc into each of next 2 sts, over last 2 sts work

sc2tog, skip tch, turn.

3rd row: As 2nd row.

4th row: 4ch, skip 1 st, 1tr into next st (counts as tr2tog), *1dc into next st, 1hdc into next st, 1sc into next st, 1hdc into next st, 1dc into next st**, over next 3 sts work tr3tog; rep from * ending last rep at **, over last 2 sts work tr2tog, skip tch, turn.

5th row: 1ch (counts as 1sc), skip 1 st, 1sc into next and each st to end, turn.

6th row: As 5th row.

Rep these 6 rows.

Single Rib

Multiple of 2 sts.

(add 2 for base chain)

Special Abbreviation: Dc/rf (raised double crochet at the front of the fabric) = Wrap the yarn around the hook, insert the hook from in front and from right to left around the stem of the appropriate stitch, and complete the stitch normally.

Dc/rb (raised double crochet at the back of the fabric) = Wrap the yarn around the hook, insert the hook from behind and from right to left around the stem of the appropriate stitch, and complete the stitch normally.

1st row (wrong side): Skip 3ch (count as 1dc), 1dc into next and each ch to end, turn.

2nd row: 2ch (count as 1dc), skip first st, *1dc/rf around next st, 1dc/rb around next st; rep from * ending 1dc into top of tch, turn.

Rep 2nd row.

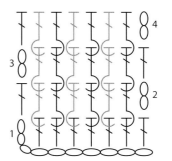

Theater Box

Multiple of 6 sts + 4.

Special Abbreviation: Puff st = [yo, insert hook into next st, yo and draw a loop through] 3 times into same st, yo and draw through 7 loops on hook, work 1 firm ch to close puff st.

1st row (right side): Work 1sc into 2nd ch from hook, 1sc into each ch to end, turn.

2nd row: 3ch (count as 1dc), skip first sc, 1dc into each sc to end, turn.

3rd row: 1ch, 1sc into each of first 2dc, *3ch, skip 2dc, 1 puff st into next dc, 3ch, skip 2dc, 1sc into next dc; rep from * to last dc, 1sc into 3rd of 3ch at beg of previous row, turn.

4th row: 5ch (count as 1dc, 2ch), work 3sc into closing ch of next puff st, *3ch, 3sc into closing ch of next puff st; rep from * to last 2sc, 2ch, 1dc into last sc, turn.

5th row: 1ch, 1sc into first dc, 2sc into first 2ch sp, *1sc into each of next 3sc, 3sc into next 3ch sp; rep from * to end working last sc into 3rd of 5ch at beg of previous row, turn.

Rep 2nd to 5th rows.

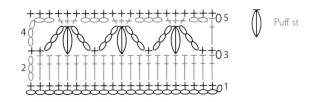

Puff st

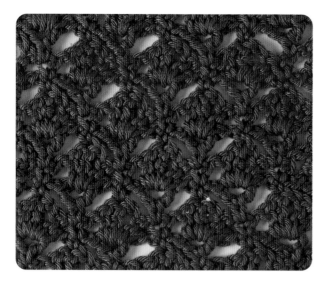

Crow's Foot Lattice

Multiple of 6 sts + 1.

(add 4 for base chain)

1st row (wrong side): Skip 4ch (count as 1tr and 1ch), 1dc into next ch, 1ch, skip 2ch, 1sc into next ch, *1ch, skip 2ch, work [1dc, 1ch, 1tr, 1ch, 1dc] into next ch, 1ch, skip 2ch, 1sc into next ch; rep from * to last 3ch, 1ch, skip 2ch, [1dc, 1ch, 1tr] into last ch, turn.

2nd row: 1ch, 1sc into first st, *1ch, skip 2 sps, 1tr into next sc, 1ch, 1dc into base of tr just made, 1ch, skip 2 sps, 1sc into next tr; rep from * ending last rep in tch, turn.

3rd row: 1ch, 1sc into first st, *1ch, skip sp, work [1dc, 1ch, 1tr, 1ch, 1dc] into next sp, 1ch, skip sp, 1sc into next sc; rep from * to end, turn.

4th row: 4ch (count as 1tr), 1dc into 4th ch from hook, *1ch, skip 2 sps, 1sc into next tr, 1ch, 1tr into next sc**, 1ch, 1dc into base of tr just made; rep from * ending last rep at **, 1dc into base of tr just made, turn.

5th row: 5ch (count as 1tr and 1ch), 1dc into first st, 1ch, skip sp, 1sc into next sc, *1ch, skip sp, work [1dc, 1ch, 1tr, 1ch, 1dc] into next sp, 1ch, skip sp, 1sc into next sc; rep from * ending 1ch, skip sp, [1dc, 1ch, 1tr] into top of tch, turn.

Rep 2nd to 5th rows.

Solid Shell Stitch

Multiple of 6 sts + 1.

(add 1 for base chain)

1st row: 1sc into 2nd ch from hook, *skip 2ch, 5dc into next ch, skip 2ch, 1sc into next ch; rep from * to end, turn.

2nd row: 3ch (count as 1dc), 2dc into first st, *skip 2dc, 1sc into next dc, skip 2dc, 5dc into next sc; rep from * ending last rep with 3dc into last sc, skip tch, turn.

3rd row: 1ch, 1sc into first st, *skip 2dc, 5dc into next sc, skip 2dc, 1sc into next dc; rep from * ending last rep with 1sc into top of tch, turn.

Rep 2nd and 3rd rows.

Wavy Shell Stitch 1

Multiple of 14 sts + 1.

(add 2 for base chain)

1st row (right side): Skip 2ch (count as 1dc), 3dc into next ch, *skip 3ch, 1sc into each of next 7ch, skip 3ch, 7dc into next ch; rep from * ending last rep with 4dc into last ch, turn.

2nd row: 1ch, 1sc into first st, 1sc into each st to end, finishing with 1sc into top of tch, turn.

3rd row: 1ch, 1sc into each of first 4 sts, *skip 3 sts, 7dc into next st, skip 3 sts, 1sc into each of next 7 sts; rep from * to last 11 sts, skip 3 sts, 7dc into next st, skip 3 sts, 1sc into each of last 4 sc, skip tch, turn.

4th row: 1ch, 1sc into first st, 1sc into next and each st to end, skip tch, turn.

5th row: 3ch (count as 1dc), 3dc into first st, *skip 3 sts, 1sc into each of next 7 sts, skip 3 sts, 7dc into next st; rep from * ending last rep with 4dc into last sc, skip tch, turn. Rep 2nd to 5th rows.

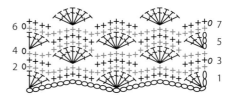

Wavy Shell Stitch II

Work as Wavy Shell Stitch I (page 112).

Work 1 row each in colors A, B, and C throughout.

Ideally, you should leave tails at least six inches long
whenever you cut your crochet thread or yarn, and when
you start your base (foundation) chain.

Wheatsheaf

Multiple of 5 sts + 2.

1st row (wrong side): Work 1sc into 2nd ch from hook, 1sc into next ch, *3ch, skip 2ch, 1sc into each of next 3ch; rep from * to end omitting 1sc at end of last rep, turn.

2nd row: 1ch, 1sc into first sc, *5dc into next 3ch arch, skip 1sc, 1sc into next sc; rep from * to end, turn.

3rd row: 3ch (count as 1hdc, 1ch), skip first 2 sts, 1sc into each of next 3dc, *3ch, skip next 3 sts, 1sc into each of next 3dc; rep from * to last 2 sts, 1ch, 1hdc into last sc, turn.

4th row: 3ch (count as 1dc), 2dc into first ch sp, skip 1sc, 1sc into next sc, *5dc into next 3ch arch, skip 1sc, 1sc into next sc; rep from * to last sp, 2dc into last sp, 1dc into 2nd of 3ch at beg of previous row, turn.

5th row: 1ch, 1sc into each of first 2dc, *3ch, skip 3 sts, 1sc into each of next 3dc; rep from * to end omitting 1sc at end of last rep and placing last sc into 3rd of 3ch at beg of previous row, turn.

Rep 2nd to 5th rows.

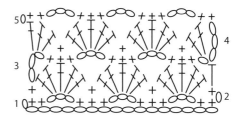

Woven Shell Stitch

Multiple of 6 sts + 1.

(add 2 for base chain)

Special Abbreviation: CGr (Crossed Group) = skip 3dc and next st, 3dc into 2nd of next 3dc, 3ch, 3dc into 2nd of 3dc just skipped working back over last 3dc made.

1st row: Skip 3ch (count as 1dc), *skip next 3ch, 3dc into next ch, 3ch, 3dc into 2nd of 3ch just skipped working back over last 3dc made, skip 1ch, 1dc into next ch; rep from * to end, turn.

2nd row: 3ch (count as 1dc), 3dc into first st, 1sc into next 3ch arch, *1CGr, 1sc into next 3ch arch; rep from * ending 4dc into top of tch, turn.

3rd row: 3ch (count as 1dc), skip 1 st, 1CGr, *1sc into next 3ch loop, 1CGr; rep from * ending 1dc into top of tch, turn.

Rep 2nd and 3rd rows.

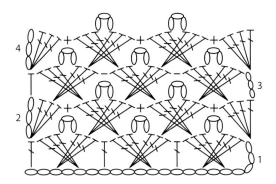

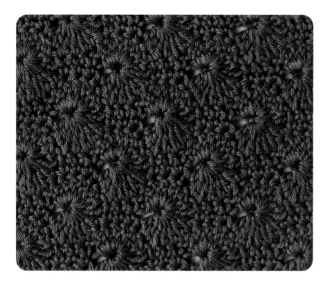

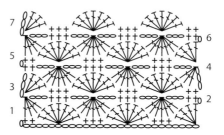

Catherine Wheel I

Multiple of 10 sts + 6.

(add 1 for base chain)

Special Abbreviation: CL (Cluster) = work [yo, insert hook, yo, draw loop through, yo, draw through 2 loops] over the number of sts indicated, yo, draw through all loops on hook.

1st row (wrong side): 1sc into 2nd ch from hook, 1sc into next ch, *skip 3ch, 7dc into next ch, skip 3ch, 1sc into each of next 3ch; rep from * to last 4 ch, skip 3 ch, 4dc into last ch, turn.

2nd row: 1ch, 1sc into first st, 1sc into next st, *3ch, 1CL over next 7 sts, 3ch, 1sc into each of next 3 sts; rep from * to last 4 sts, 3ch, 1CL over last 4 sts, skip tch, turn.

3rd row: 3ch (count as 1dc), 3dc into first st, *skip 3ch, 1sc into each of next 3sc, skip 3ch, 7dc into loop that closed next CL; rep from * to end finishing with skip 3ch, 1sc into each of last 2sc, skip tch, turn.

4th row: 3ch (count as 1dc), skip first st, 1CL over next 3 sts, *3ch, 1sc into each of next 3 sts, 3ch, 1CL over next 7 sts; rep from * finishing with 3ch, 1sc into next st, 1sc into top of tch, turn.

5th row: 1ch, 1sc into each of first 2sc, *skip 3ch, 7dc into loop that closed next CL, skip 3ch, 1sc into each of next 3sc; rep from * ending skip 3ch, 4dc into top of tch, turn. Rep 2nd to 5th rows.

Catherine Wheel II

Work as Catherine Wheel I (page 116).
Make base chain and work first row in color A. Thereafter,
work 2 rows each in color B and color A.

Catherine Wheel III

Work as Catherine Wheel I (page 116).
Work 1 row each in colors A, B, and C throughout.

To weave in loose ends, when finishing use a tapestry needle
or bodkin (a big sewing needle with a large eye and blunt tip)
rather than your crochet hook.

Catherine Wheel IV

Multiple of 8 sts +1.

(add 1 for base chain)

Special Abbreviation: CL (Cluster) worked as under Catherine Wheel I (page 116).

1st row (right side): 1sc into 2nd ch from hook, *skip 3ch, 9dc into next ch, skip 3ch, 1sc into next ch; rep from * to end, turn.

2nd row: 3ch (count as 1dc), skip first st, 1CL over next 4 sts, *3ch, 1sc into next st, 3ch, 1CL over next 9 sts; rep from * ending last rep with 1CL over last 5 sts, skip tch, turn.

3rd row: 3ch (count as 1dc), 4dc into first st, *skip 3ch, 1sc into next sc, skip 3ch, 9dc into loop that closed next CL; rep from * ending last rep with 5dc into top of tch, turn.

4th row: 1ch, 1sc into first st, *3ch, 1CL over next 9 sts, 3ch, 1sc into next st; rep from * ending last rep with 1sc into top of tch, turn.

5th row: 1ch, 1sc into first st, *skip 3ch, 9dc into loop that closed next CL, skip 3ch, 1sc into next sc; rep from * to end, skip tch, turn.

Rep 2nd to 5th rows.

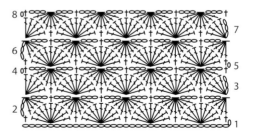

Smooth Wave Stitch

Multiple of 8 sts + 4.

(add 1 for base chain)

Work 2 rows each in colors A and B alternately throughout.

1st row (right side): Skip 2ch (count as 1sc), 1sc into each of next 3ch, *1dc into each of next 4ch, 1sc into each of next 4ch; rep from * to end, turn.

2nd row: 1ch (counts as 1sc), skip first st, 1sc into each of next 3 sts, *1dc into each of next 4 sts, 1sc into each of next 4 sts; rep from * to end working last st into top of tch, turn.

3rd row: 3ch (count as 1dc), skip first st, 1dc into each of next 3 sts, *1sc into each of next 4 sts, 1dc into each of next 4 sts; rep from * to end working last st into top of tch, turn.

4th row: As 3rd row.

5th and 6th rows: As 2nd row.

Rep 3rd to 6th rows.

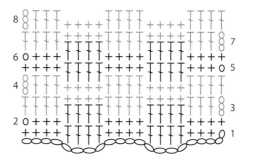

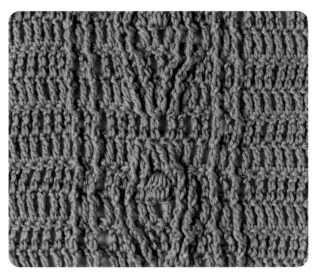

Silt Stitch

Multiple of 3 sts + 1.

(add 2 for base chain)

1st row (right side): Skip 3ch (count as 1dc), 1dc into next and each ch to end, turn.

2nd row: 1ch (counts as 1sc), 2dc into first st, *skip 2 sts, work [1sc, 2dc] into next st; rep from * to last 3 sts, skip 2 sts, 1sc into top of tch, turn.

3rd row: 3ch (count as 1dc), skip 1 st, 1dc into next and each st to end, working last st into top of tch, turn.

Rep 2nd and 3rd rows.

Tulip Cable

Worked over 15 sts on a background of basic double crochets with any number of sts.

Special Abbreviations

FCL (Forward Cluster) = leaving last loop of each st on hook, work 1dc into next st and 1tr/rf or rb (see Note below) around next st after that, ending yo, draw through all 3 loops on hook.

BCL (Backward Cluster) = leaving last loop of each st on hook, work 1tr/rf or rb around st below dc just made and 1dc into next st.

Note: Raised legs of these clusters are to be worked at front (rf) on right-side rows and at back (rb) on wrong-side rows as indicated in the text thus: FCL/rf, FCL/rb, BCL/rf, BCL/rb.

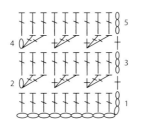

TCL (Triple Cluster) = leaving last loop of each st on hook work, 1tr/rf around st below dc just made, 1dc/rf around next Puff st, and 1tr/rf around next st, ending yo, draw through all 4 loops on hook.

1st row (right side): 1tr/rf around next st, 1dc into next st, 1tr/rf around next st, 1dc into each of next 2sts, [1FCL/rf] twice, 1dc into next st, [1BCL/rf] twice, 1dc into each of next 2 sts, 1tr/rf around next st, 1dc into next st, 1tr/rf around next st.

2nd row: [1tr/rb around next st, 1dc into next st] twice, [1FCL/rb] twice, 1dc into each of next 3 sts, [1BCL/rb] twice, [1dc into next st, 1tr/rb around next st] twice.

3rd row: [1tr/rf around next st, 1dc into next st] twice, 1tr/rf around each of next 2 sts, 1dc into each of next 3 sts, 1tr/rf around each of next 2 sts, [1dc into next st, 1tr/rf around next st] twice.

4th row: 1tr/rb around next st, 1dc into next st, 1tr/rb around next st, 1dc into each of next 2 sts, [1BCL/rb] twice, work a Puff st of hdc5tog all into next st, [1FCL/rb] twice, 1dc into each of next 2 sts, 1tr/rb around next st, 1dc into next st, 1tr/rb around next st.

5th row: 1tr/rf around next st, 1dc into next st, 1tr/rf around next st, 1dc into each of next 3 sts, 1BCL/rf, 1TCL, 1FCL/rf, 1dc into each of next 3 sts, 1tr/rf around next st, 1dc into next st, 1tr/rf around next st.

6th row: *1tr/rb around next st, 1dc into next st, 1tr/rb around next st**, 1dc into each of next 9 sts, rep from * to **.

Rep these 6 rows.

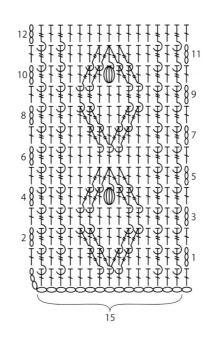

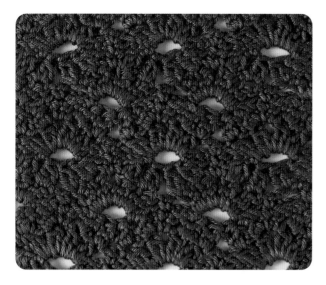

Petal Pattern I

Multiple of 11 sts + 3.

Special Abbreviation: Dc2tog = work 2dc into next st until 1 loop of each remains on hook, yo and through all 3 loops on hook.

1st row (right side): Work 1sc into 2nd ch from hook, 1ch, skip 1ch, 1sc into next ch, [3ch, skip 3ch, 1sc into next ch] twice, *2ch, skip 2ch, 1sc into next ch, [3ch, skip 3ch, 1sc into next ch] twice; rep from * to last 2ch, 1ch, skip 1ch, 1sc into last ch, turn.

2nd row: 3ch (count as 1dc), into first ch sp work [dc2tog, 2ch, dc2tog], 1ch, skip 1sc, 1sc into next sc, *1ch, skip 3ch sp, dc2tog into next 2ch sp, into same sp as last dc2tog work [2ch, dc2tog] 3 times, 1ch, skip 3ch sp, 1sc into next sc; rep from * to last 2 sps, 1ch, skip 3ch sp, into

last ch sp work [dc2tog, 2ch, dc2tog], 1dc into last sc, turn.

3rd row: 1ch, 1sc into first dc, *3ch, work 1dc2tog into top of each of next 4dc2tog, 3ch, 1sc into next 2ch sp; rep from * to end placing last sc into 3rd of 3ch at beg of previous row, turn.

4th row: 1ch, 1sc into first sc, *3ch, 1sc into top of next dc2tog, 2ch, skip 2dc2tog, 1sc into top of next dc2tog, 3ch, 1sc into next sc; rep from * to end, turn.

5th row: 1ch, work 1sc into first sc, *1ch, skip 3ch sp, dc2tog into next 2ch sp, into same sp as last dc2tog work [2ch, dc2tog] 3 times, 1ch, skip 3ch sp, 1sc into next sc; rep from * to end, turn.

6th row: 3ch, work 1dc2tog into top of each of next 2dc2tog, 3ch, 1sc into next 2ch sp, 3ch, *dc2tog into top of next 4dc2tog, 3ch, 1sc into next 2ch sp, 3ch; rep from * to last 2dc2tog, work 1dc2tog into each of last 2dc2tog, 1dc into last sc, turn.

7th row: 1ch, 1sc into first dc, 1ch, skip 1dc2tog, 1sc into next dc2tog, 3ch, 1sc into next sc, 3ch, *1sc into top of next dc2tog, 2ch, skip 2dc2tog, 1sc into top of next dc2tog, 3ch, 1sc into next sc, 3ch; rep from * to last 2dc2tog, 1sc into next dc2tog, 1ch, skip 1dc2tog, 1sc into 3rd of 3ch at beg of previous row, turn.

Rep 2nd to 7th rows.

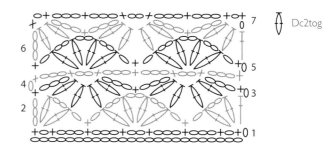

Petal Pattern II

Work as Petal Pattern I (page 122) **but** working 1st and 2nd rows in A, then 3 rows each in B and A throughout. **Note:** Cut yarn after each color change.

Petal Pattern III

Work as Petal Pattern I (page 122) **but** working 1st and 2nd rows in A, then work 3 rows each in B, C, and A throughout.

To weave ends in, thread a tapestry needle with the end of the yarn. Sew back through a few stitches, previous rows or rounds of stitches to secure the end. For the most professional results, weave in your loose ends roughly 2 inches forward and then 2 inches in the opposite direction.

Zig-Zag Double String Network

Multiple of 6 sts + 1.

(add 1 for base chain)

Base row (right side): 1sc into 2nd ch from hook, *5ch, skip 5ch, 1sc into next ch; rep from * to end, turn.

Commence Pattern

1st row: 1ch, 1sc into first st, *5ch, skip 5ch, 1sc into next sc; rep from * to end, skip tch, turn.

2nd row: 1ch, 1sc into first st, *7ch, skip 5ch, 1sc into next sc; rep from * to end, skip tch, turn.

3rd row: 1ch, 1sc into first st, *7ch, skip 7ch, 1sc into next sc; rep from * to end, skip tch, turn.

4th row: 5ch (count as 1dc and 2ch), inserting hook under the 7ch arch made in the 2nd row, work 1sc thus binding the arches of the 2nd and 3rd rows together, *5ch, 1sc under next pair of arches as before; rep from * ending 2ch, 1dc into last sc, skip tch, turn.

5th row: 1ch, 1sc into first st, 2ch, skip 2ch, 1sc into next sc, *5ch, skip 5ch, 1sc into next sc; rep from * ending 2ch, skip next 2ch of tch, 1sc into next ch, turn.

6th row: 6ch (count as 1dc and 3ch), skip 2ch, 1sc into next sc, *7ch, skip 5ch, 1sc into next sc; rep from * ending 3ch, skip 2ch, 1dc into last sc, skip tch, turn.

7th row: 1ch, 1sc into first st, 3ch, skip 3ch, 1sc into next sc, *7ch, skip 7ch, 1sc into next sc; rep from * ending 3ch, skip next 3ch of tch, 1sc into next ch, turn.

8th row: 1ch, 1sc into first st, *5ch, 1sc under next pair of arches together; rep from * ending last rep with 1sc into last sc, skip tch, turn.

Rep these 8 rows.

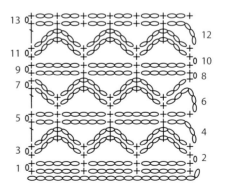

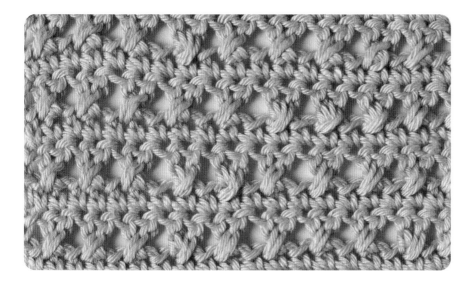

Crossed Double Crochet Stitch

Multiple of 2 sts.

(add 2 for base chain)

Special Abbreviation: 2Cdc (2 crossed double crochets) worked as under Textured Wave Stitch (page 93).

1st row (right side): Skip 3ch (count as 1dc), *2Cdc over next 2ch; rep from * ending 1dc into last ch, turn.

2nd row: 1ch (counts as 1sc), skip 1 st, 1sc into next and each st to end, working last st into top of tch, turn.

3rd row: 3ch (count as 1dc), skip 1st, *work 2Cdc over next 2 sts; rep from * ending 1dc into tch, turn.

Rep 2nd and 3rd rows.

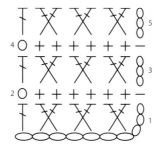

Crosshatch Stitch I

Multiple of 7 sts + 4.

(add 3 for base chain)

1st row: Skip 2ch (count as 1dc), 2dc into next ch, *skip 3ch, 1sc into next ch, 3ch, 1dc into each of next 3ch; rep from * to last 4ch, skip 3ch, 1sc into last ch, turn.

2nd row: 3ch (count as 1dc), 2dc into first sc, *skip 3dc, 1sc into first of 3ch, 3ch, 1dc into each of next 2ch, 1dc into next sc; rep from * ending skip 2dc, 1sc into top of tch, turn.

Rep 2nd row.

Crosshatch Stitch II

Work as Crosshatch Stitch I (this page).

Work 1 row each in colors A, B, and C throughout.

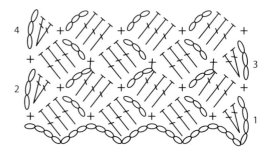

Zig-Zag Rib

Multiple of 4 sts + 2.

(add 2 for base chain)

Special Abbreviation: Dc/rf (raised double crochet at the front of the fabric) = Wrap the yarn around the hook, insert the hook from in front and from right to left around the stem of the appropriate stitch, and complete the stitch normally.

Dc/rb (raised double crochet at the back of the fabric) = Wrap the yarn around the hook, insert the hook from behind and from right to left around the stem of the appropriate stitch, and complete the stitch normally.

Base row (wrong side): Skip 3ch (count as 1dc), 1dc into next and each ch to end, turn.

Commence Pattern

1st row: 2ch (count as 1dc), skip first st, *1dc/rf around

each of next 2 sts, 1dc/rb around each of next 2 sts; rep from * ending 1dc into top of tch, turn.

2nd row: 2ch (count as 1dc), skip first st, 1dc/rb around next st, *1dc/rf around each of next 2 sts**, 1dc/rb around each of next 2 sts; rep from * ending last rep at ** when 2 sts remain, 1dc/rb around next st, 1dc into top of tch, turn.

3rd row: 2ch (count as 1dc), skip first st, *1dc/rb around each of next 2 sts, 1dc/rf around each of next 2 sts; rep from * ending 1dc into top of tch, turn.

4th row: 2ch (count as 1dc), skip first st, 1dc/rf around next st, *1dc/rb around each of next 2 sts**, 1dc/rf around each of next 2 sts; rep from * ending last rep at ** when 2 sts remain, 1dc/rf around next st, 1dc into top of tch, turn.

5th row: As 3rd row.

6th row: As 2nd row.

7th row: As 1st row.

8th row: As 4th row.

Rep these 8 rows.

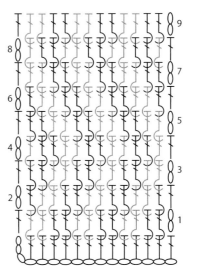

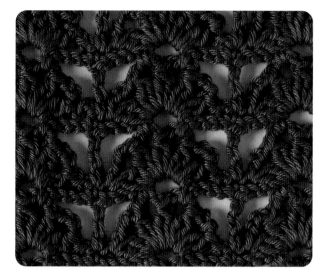

Dc2tog

Flame Stitch

Multiple of 10 sts + 2.

Special Abbreviation: Dc2tog = work 2dc into next 3ch arch until 1 loop of each remains on hook, yo and through all 3 loops on hook.

1st row (wrong side): Work 1sc into 2nd ch from hook, *3ch, skip 3ch, 1sc into next ch, 3ch, skip 1ch, 1sc into next ch, 3ch, skip 3ch, 1sc into next ch; rep from * to end, turn.

2nd row: 1ch, 1sc into first sc, *1ch, skip next 3ch sp, dc2tog into next 3ch arch, into same arch as last dc2tog work [3ch, dc2tog] 4 times, 1ch, skip next 3ch sp, 1sc into next sc; rep from * to end, turn.

3rd row: 7ch (count as 1tr, 3ch), skip next 3ch arch, 1sc into next 3ch arch, 3ch, 1sc into next 3ch arch, 3ch, 1tr into next sc, *3ch, skip next 3ch arch, 1sc into next 3ch arch, 3ch, 1sc into next 3ch arch, 3ch, 1tr into next sc; rep from * to end, turn.

4th row: 1ch, 1sc into first tr, *1ch, skip next 3ch sp, dc2tog into next 3ch arch, into same arch as last dc2tog work [3ch, dc2tog] 4 times, 1ch, 1sc into next tr; rep from * to end, working last sc into 4th of 7ch at beg of previous row, turn.

Rep 3rd and 4th rows.

Trinity Stitch I

Multiple of 2 sts + 1.

(add 1 for base chain)

1st row: 1sc into 2nd ch from hook, sc3tog inserting hook first into same ch as previous sc, then into each of next 2ch, *1ch, sc3tog inserting hook first into same ch as 3rd leg of previous cluster, then into each of next 2ch; rep from * to last ch, 1sc into same ch as 3rd leg of previous cluster, turn.

2nd row: 1ch, 1sc into first st, sc3tog inserting hook first into same place as previous sc, then into top of next cluster, then into next ch sp, *1ch, sc3tog inserting hook first into same ch sp as 3rd leg of previous cluster, then into top of next cluster, then into next ch sp; rep from * to end working 3rd leg of last cluster into last sc, 1sc into same place, skip tch, turn.

Rep 2nd row.

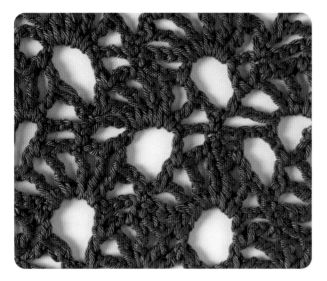

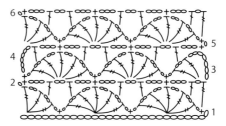

Open Fan Stitch

Multiple of 10 sts + 6.

(add 1 for base chain)

1st row (right side): 1sc into 2nd ch from hook, *1ch, skip 4ch, into next ch work a Fan of 1tr, [2ch, 1tr] 4 times, then 1ch, skip 4ch, 1sc into next ch; rep from * to last 5ch, 1ch, skip 4ch, into last ch work [1tr, 2ch] twice and 1tr, turn.

2nd row: 1ch, 1sc into first st, *3ch, skip next 2ch sp, 1dc into next sp**, 2ch, skip next tr, sc and tr and work 1dc into first 2ch sp of next Fan, 3ch, work 1sc into center tr of Fan; rep from * ending last rep at **, 1ch, 1tr into last sc, skip tch, turn.

3rd row: 7ch (count as 1tr and 2ch), skip first tr, work [1tr, 2ch, 1tr] into next 1ch sp, 1ch, skip 3ch sp, 1sc into next sc, *1ch, skip next 3ch sp, work a Fan into next 2ch sp, 1ch, skip next 3ch sp, 1sc into next sc; rep from * to end, skip tch, turn.

4th row: 6ch (count as 1tr and 1ch), skip first tr, work 1dc into next 2ch sp, 3ch, 1sc into center tr of Fan, *3ch, skip next 2ch sp, 1dc into next 2ch sp, 2ch, skip next tr, sc and tr, work 1dc into next 2ch sp, 3ch, 1sc into center tr of Fan; rep from * ending last rep in 3rd ch of tch, turn.

5th row: 1ch, *1sc into sc, 1ch, skip next 3ch sp, Fan into next 2ch sp, 1ch, skip next 3ch sp; rep from * to last sc, 1sc into sc, 1ch, skip next 3ch sp, work [1tr, 2ch] twice and 1tr all into top of tch, turn.

Rep 2nd to 5th rows.

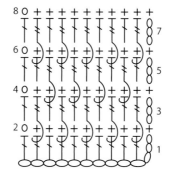

Ripple Stitch I

Multiple of 2 sts +1.

(add 2 for base chain)

Special Abbreviation: Tr/rf (raised treble crochet at the front of the fabric) = Wrap the yarn around the hook, insert the hook from in front and from right to left around the stem of the appropriate stitch, and complete the stitch normally.

Tr/rb (raised treble crochet at the back of the fabric) = Wrap the yarn around the hook, insert the hook from behind and from right to left around the stem of the appropriate stitch, and complete the stitch normally.

1st row (right side): Skip 3ch (count as 1dc), 1dc into each ch to end, turn.

2nd row: 1ch (counts as 1sc), skip first st, 1sc into each st to end, working last st into top of tch, turn.

3rd row: 3ch (count as 1dc), skip first st, *1tr/rf around dc below next st, 1dc into next st; rep from * to end, turn.

4th row: As 2nd row.

5th row: 3ch (count as 1dc), skip first st, *1dc into next st, 1tr/rf around dc below next st; rep from * to last 2 sts, 1dc into each of last 2 sts, turn.

Rep 2nd to 5th rows.

Ripple Stitch II

Work as Ripple Stitch I (page 131).
Work 2 rows each in colors A and B alternately
throughout.

Crochet doesn't have to be expensive. Because of its very
nature, one can use odd balls of yarn bought in sales,
left-over yarns from previous projects, and recycled materials.

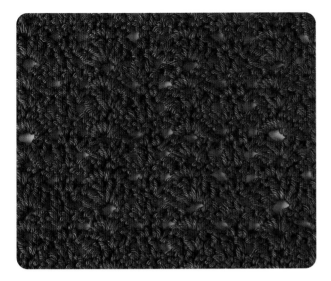

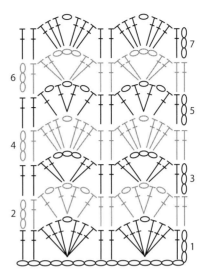

Rack Stitch

Multiple of 7 sts + 4.

1st row (right side): Work 1dc into 4th ch from hook, *skip 2ch, into next ch work [3dc, 1ch, 3dc], skip 2ch, 1dc into each of next 2ch; rep from * to end, turn.

2nd row: 3ch (count as 1dc), skip first dc, 1dc into next dc, *skip 2dc, 1dc into next dc, 1ch, into next ch sp work [1dc, 1ch, 1dc], 1ch, 1dc into next dc, skip 2dc, 1dc into each of next 2dc; rep from * to end placing last dc into 3rd of 3ch at beg of previous row, turn.

3rd row: 3ch, skip first dc, 1dc into next dc, *skip next ch sp, into next ch sp work [2dc, 3ch, 2dc], skip 2dc, 1dc into each of next 2dc; rep from * to end placing last dc into 3rd of 3ch at beg of previous row, turn.

4th row: 3ch, skip first dc, 1dc into next dc, * into next 3ch sp work [3dc, 1ch, 3dc], skip 2dc, 1dc into each of next 2dc; rep from * to end placing last dc into 3rd of 3ch at beg of previous row, turn.

Rep 2nd to 4th rows.

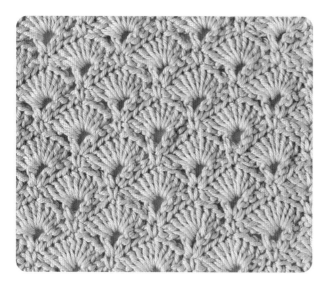

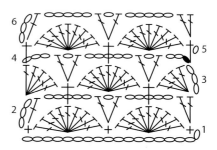

Fan and V Stitch

Multiple of 8 sts + 1.

(add 1 for base chain)

1st row (right side): 1sc into 2nd ch from hook, *skip 3ch, 9dc into next ch, skip 3ch, 1sc into next ch; rep from * to end, turn.

2nd row: 3ch (count as 1dc), 1dc into first st, *5ch, skip 9dc group, work a V st of [1dc, 1ch, 1dc] into next sc; rep from * ending 5ch, skip last 9dc group, 2dc into last sc, skip tch, turn.

3rd row: 3ch (count as 1dc), 4dc into first st, *working over next 5ch so as to enclose it, work 1sc into 5th dc of group in row below**, 9dc into sp at center of next V st; rep from * ending last rep at **, 5dc into top of tch, turn.

4th row: 3ch, skip 5dc, V st into next sc, *5ch, skip 9dc group, V st into next sc; rep from * ending 2ch, sl st to top of tch, turn.

5th row: 1ch, 1sc over sl st into first st of row below, *9dc into sp at center of next V st**, working over next 5ch so as to enclose it work 1sc into 5th dc of group in row below; rep from * ending last rep at **, 1sc into first ch of tch, turn.

Rep 2nd to 5th rows.

End with a wrong-side row, working [2ch, sl st to 5th dc of group, 2ch] in place of 5ch between the V sts.

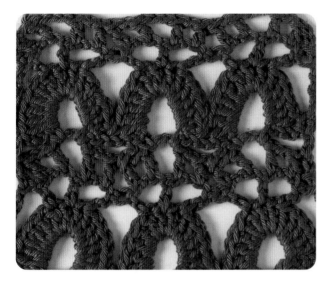

Norman Arch Stitch

Multiple of 9 sts + 1.

(add 1 for base chain)

1st row (wrong side): 1sc into 2nd ch from hook, *3ch, skip 3ch, 1sc into next ch, 7ch, 1sc into next ch, 3ch, skip 3ch, 1sc into next ch; rep from * to end, turn.

2nd row: 1ch, 1sc into first sc, *skip 3ch, work 13dc into next 7ch arch, skip 3ch, 1sc into next st; rep from * to end, skip tch, turn.

3rd row: 5ch (count as 1dtr), skip first sc and next 5dc, *[1dc into next dc, 3ch] twice, 1dc into next dc**, skip [next 5dc, 1sc and 5dc]; rep from * ending last rep at **, skip next 5dc, 1dtr into last sc, skip tch, turn.

4th row: 3ch (count as 1dc), skip first st and next dc, *1dc into next ch, 1ch, skip 1ch, 1dc into next ch, 3ch, skip 1dc, 1dc into next ch, 1ch, skip 1ch, 1dc into next ch**, skip next 2dc; rep from * ending last rep at **, skip next dc, 1dc into top of tch, turn.

5th row: 6ch (count as 1dc and 3ch), *skip next 1ch sp, work [1sc, 7ch, 1sc] into next 3ch sp, 3ch, skip next 1ch sp**, 1dc between next 2dc, 3ch; rep from * ending last rep at **, 1dc into top of tch, turn.

Rep 2nd to 5th rows.

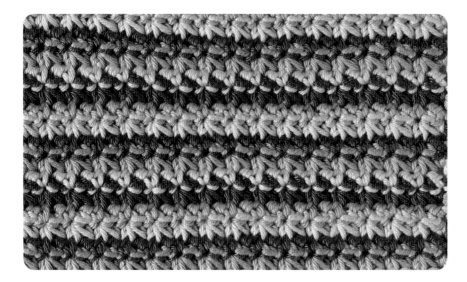

Trinity Stitch II

Work as Trinity Stitch I (page 129).

Work 1 row each in colors A, B, and C throughout.

Note: Normally the maximum number of stitches that may be worked together into a single crochet cluster is 3. (Longer stitches may have more.) Remember that working stitches together into clusters is often the best way to decrease.

Refresh your wardrobe by creating new garments and accessories in crochet to complement favorite woven pieces. Use ribbon, decorative bindings, and printed and gingham fabric cut into strips to give an unusual twist to crochet stitches.

Crossbill Stitch

Multiple of 4 sts + 1.

(add 2 for base chain)

Special Abbreviation: 2Cdc (2 crossed double crochets)
= skip 2 sts, 1dc into next st, 1ch, 1dc into first of 2 sts
just skipped working back over last dc made.

1st row: Skip 3ch (count as 1dc), *work 2Cdc over next
3ch, 1dc into next ch; rep from * to end, turn.

2nd row: 3ch (count as 1dc), 1dc into first st, skip 1dc,
*1dc into next ch, work 2Cdc over next 3dc, rep from *
ending 1dc into last ch, skip 1dc, 2dc into top of tch, turn.

3rd row: 3ch (count as 1dc), skip 1 st, *work 2Cdc over
next 3dc, 1dc into next ch; rep from * ending last rep into
top of tch, turn.

Rep 2nd and 3rd rows.

Commence Pattern

1st row: 2ch (count as 1dc), skip first st, *1dc/rf around each of next 4 sts, 1dc/rb around each of next 4 sts; rep from * ending 1dc into top of tch, turn.

Rep the last row 3 times.

5th row: 2ch (count as 1dc), skip first st, *1dc/rb around each of next 4 sts, 1dc/rf around each of next 4 sts; rep from * ending 1dc into top of tch, turn.

Rep the last row 3 times.

Rep these 8 rows.

Basketweave Stitch

Multiple of 8 sts + 2.

(add 2 for base chain)

Special Abbreviation: Dc/rf (raised double crochet at the front of the fabric) = Wrap the yarn around the hook, insert the hook from in front and from right to left around the stem of the appropriate stitch, and complete the stitch normally.

Dc/rb (raised double crochet at the back of the fabric) = Wrap the yarn around the hook, insert the hook from behind and from right to left around the stem of the appropriate stitch, and complete the stitch normally.

Base row (wrong side): Skip 3ch (count as 1dc), 1dc into next and each ch to end, turn.

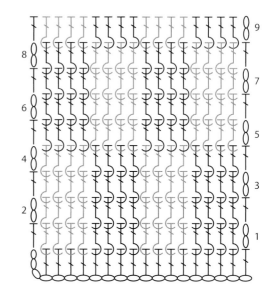

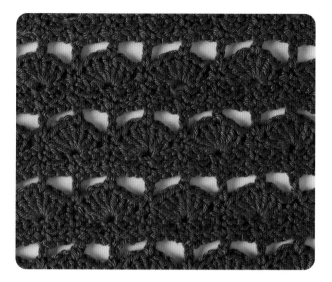

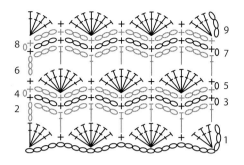

Cool Design

Multiple of 8 sts + 4.

1st row (right side): Work 3dc into 4th ch from hook, skip 3ch, 1sc into next ch, *skip 3ch, 7dc into next ch, skip 3ch, 1sc into next ch; rep from * to last 4ch, skip 3ch, 4dc into last ch, turn.

2nd row: 6ch (count as 1dc, 3ch), 1dc into next sc, *3ch, skip 3dc, 1dc into next dc, 3ch, 1dc into next sc; rep from * to last 4 sts, 3ch, 1dc into top of 3ch at beg of previous row, turn.

3rd row: 1ch, *1sc into next dc, 3ch; rep from * to last st, 1sc into 3rd of 6ch at beg of previous row, turn.

4th row: 1ch, 1sc into first sc, *3ch, 1sc into next sc; rep from * to end, turn.

5th row: 1ch, 1sc into first sc, *7dc into next sc, 1sc into next sc; rep from * to end, turn.

6th row: 6ch, skip 3dc, 1dc into next dc, 3ch, 1dc into next sc, *3ch, skip 3dc, 1dc into next dc, 3ch, 1dc into next sc; rep from * to end, turn.

7th and 8th rows: As 3rd and 4th rows.

9th row: 3ch (count as 1dc), 3dc into first sc, 1sc into next sc, *7dc into next sc, 1sc into next sc; rep from * to last sc, 4dc into last sc, turn.

Rep 2nd to 9th rows.

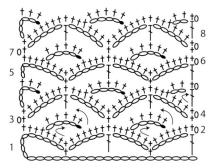

Double Arch Ground

Multiple of 10 sts + 1.

(add 8 for base chain)

1st row (wrong side): 1sc into 14th ch from hook, *5ch, skip 4ch, 1dc into next ch**, 5ch, skip 4ch, 1sc into next ch; rep from * ending last rep at **, turn.

2nd row: 1ch, 1sc into first dc, *6sc into next 5ch arch, 1sc into next sc, 3sc into beginning of next 5ch arch, work a "back double" of [4ch, then without turning work, skip 6 previous sc and work a sl st back into previous sc, now work 5sc in the normal direction into 4ch arch just worked], 3sc into remaining part of 5ch arch**, 1sc into next dc; rep from * ending last rep at **, 1sc into next ch, turn.

3rd row: 1ch, 1sc into first st, *5ch, 1dc into 3rd of 5sc of next "back double", 5ch, 1sc into sc over dc of previous row; rep from * ending last rep in last sc, turn.

4th row: 1ch, 1sc into first st, 3sc into beginning of next 5ch arch, turn, 2ch, skip 3 previous sc, work 1dc into first sc, 1ch, turn, 1sc into dc, 2sc into 2ch arch, 3sc into remaining part of 5ch arch, *1sc into next dc, 6sc into next 5ch arch, 1sc into next sc**, 3sc into beginning of 5ch arch, 1 "back double" as before, 3sc into remaining part of 5ch arch; rep from * ending last rep at **, 5ch, skip 3 previous sc, sl st back into next sc, 3sc in normal direction into beginning of 5ch arch, turn.

5th row: 8ch, *1sc into sc over dc of previous row, 5ch**, 1dc into 3rd of 5sc of next "back double", 5ch; rep from * ending last rep at **, 1dc into last sc, skip tch, turn.

Rep 2nd to 5th rows.

Sidesaddle Cluster Stitch

Multiple of 5 sts + 1.

(add 1 for base chain)

1st row: 1sc into 2nd ch from hook, *3ch, dc4tog over next 4ch, 1ch, 1sc into next ch; rep from * to end, turn.

2nd row: 5ch, 1sc into next cluster, *3ch, dc4tog all into next 3ch arch, 1ch, 1sc into next cluster; rep from * ending 3ch, dc4tog all into next 3ch arch, 1dc into last sc, skip tch, turn.

3rd row: 1ch, skip 1 st, 1sc into next CL, *3ch, 1CL into next 3ch arch, 1ch, 1sc into next CL; rep from * ending last rep with 1sc into tch arch, turn.

Rep 2nd and 3rd rows.

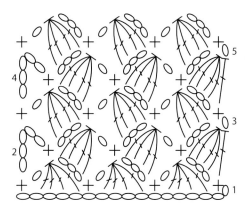

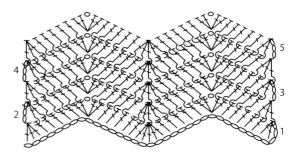

Raised Chevron Stitch

Multiple of 16 sts + 1.

(add 2 for base chain)

Special Abbreviation: Dc/rf (raised double crochet at the front of the fabric) = Wrap the yarn around the hook, insert the hook from in front and from right to left around the stem of the appropriate stitch, and complete the stitch normally.

Dc/rb (raised double crochet at the back of the fabric) = Wrap the yarn around the hook, insert the hook from behind and from right to left around the stem of the appropriate stitch, and complete the stitch normally.

1st row (right side): Skip 3ch, dc2tog over next 2ch (counts as dc3tog), *1dc into each of next 5ch, [2dc, 1ch, 2dc] into next ch, 1dc into each of next 5ch**, dc5tog over next 5ch; rep from * ending last rep at ** when 3ch remain, dc3tog, turn.

2nd row: 3ch, skip first st, dc/rb2tog over next 2 sts (all counts as dc/rb3tog), *1dc/rf around each of next 5 sts, [2dc, 1ch, 2dc] into next ch sp, 1dc/rf around each of next 5 sts**, dc/rb5tog over next 5 sts; rep from * ending last rep at ** when 3 sts remain, dc/rb3tog, turn.

3rd row: 3ch, skip first st, dc/rf2tog over next 2 sts (all counts as dc/rf3tog), *1dc/rb around each of next 5 sts, [2dc, 1ch, 2dc] into next ch sp, 1dc/rb around each of next 5 sts**, dc/rf5tog over next 5 sts; rep from * ending last rep at ** when 3 sts remain, dc/rf3tog, turn.

Rep 2nd and 3rd rows.

Garland Pattern

Multiple of 8 sts + 2.

1st row (right side): Work 1sc into 2nd ch from hook, *skip 3ch, into next ch work [1dc, 1ch, 1dc, 3ch, 1dc, 1ch, 1dc], skip 3ch, 1sc into next ch; rep from * to end, turn.

2nd row: 7ch (count as 1tr, 3ch), *skip 1ch sp, into next 3ch sp work [1sc, 3ch, 1sc], 3ch, 1tr into next sc, 3ch; rep from * to end omitting 3ch at end of last rep, turn.

3rd row: 4ch (count as 1dc, 1ch), into first tr work [1dc, 1ch, 1dc], skip 3ch sp, 1sc into next 3ch sp, *into next tr work [1dc, 1ch, 1dc, 3ch, 1dc, 1ch, 1dc], skip 3ch sp, 1sc into next 3ch sp; rep from * to last sp, skip 3ch, 1dc into next ch, work [1ch, 1dc] twice into same ch as last dc, turn.

4th row: 1ch, 1sc into first dc, 1sc into first ch sp, 3ch, 1tr into next sc, *3ch, skip 1ch sp, into next 3ch sp work [1sc, 3ch, 1sc], 3ch, 1tr into next sc; rep from * to last 3dc, 3ch, skip 1ch sp, 1sc into each of next 2ch, turn.

5th row: 1ch, 1sc into first sc, *into next tr work [1dc, 1ch, 1dc, 3ch, 1dc, 1ch, 1dc], skip 3ch sp, 1sc into next 3ch sp; rep from * to end placing last sc into last sc, turn.

Rep 2nd to 5th rows.

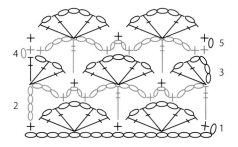

Tortoise Shell

Multiple of 5 sts + 2.

1st row (wrong side): Work 1sc into 2nd ch from hook, *5ch, skip 4ch, 1sc into next ch; rep from * to end, turn.

2nd row: 5ch (count as 1tr, 1ch), *into next 5ch arch work [1tr, 1dc, 4ch, sl st into 4th ch from hook, 1dc, 1tr], 2ch; rep from * to end omitting 1ch at end of last rep, 1tr into last sc, turn.

3rd row: 1ch, 1sc into first tr, *5ch, 1sc into next 2ch sp; rep from * to end placing last sc into 4th of 5ch at beg of previous row, turn.

Rep 2nd and 3rd rows.

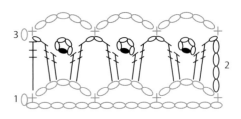

Hexagon Stitch

Multiple of 8 sts + 4.

(add 1 for base chain)

Special Abbreviations: CL (Cluster) = work [yo, insert hook, yo, draw loop through loosely] over number and position of sts indicated, ending yo, draw through all loops, 1ch tightly to close Cluster.

Picot = 5ch, 1sc into 2nd ch from hook, 1sc into each of next 3ch.

1st row (wrong side): 1sc into 2nd ch from hook, 1sc into each of next 3ch (counts as Picot), skip 3ch, 3dc into next ch, skip 3ch, 1sc into next ch, *skip 3ch, into next ch work [3dc, 1 Picot, 3dc], skip 3ch, 1sc into next ch; rep from * to end, turn.

2nd row: 4ch (count as 1tr), 1CL over each of first 8 sts, 3ch, 1sc into top of Picot, *3ch, 1CL over next 15 sts inserting hook into underside of each of 4ch of Picot, into next 3dc, 1sc, 3dc and 4sc of next Picot, then 3ch, 1sc into top of Picot; rep from * to end, turn.

3rd row: 1ch, 1sc into first st, *skip 3ch, into loop that closed next CL work [3dc, 1 Picot, 3dc], skip 3ch, 1sc into next sc; rep from * ending skip 3ch, 4dc into loop that closed last CL, skip tch, turn.

4th row: 7ch (count as 1tr and 3ch), starting into 5th ch from hook work 1CL over next 15 sts as before, *3ch, 1sc into top of Picot, 3ch, 1CL over next 15 sts; rep from * ending last rep with 1CL over last 8 sts, skip tch, turn.

5th row: 8ch, 1sc into 2nd ch from hook, 1sc into each of next 3ch (counts as 1dc and 1 Picot), 3dc into first st, skip 3ch, 1sc into next sc, *skip 3ch, into loop that closed next CL work [3dc, 1 Picot, 3dc], skip 3ch, 1sc into next sc; rep from * ending last rep with 1sc into 4th ch of tch, turn.

Rep 2nd to 5th rows.

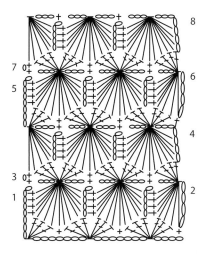

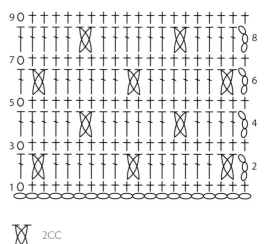

2CC

Crossed Cluster Stitch

Multiple of 8 sts + 4.

(add 1 for base chain)

Special Abbreviation: 2CC (2 crossed clusters) = skip 1 st, into next st work *[yo, insert hook, yo, draw loop through] twice, yo, draw through all 5 loops on hook; rep from * into st just skipped, working over previous cluster.

1st row (wrong side): Skip 2ch (count as 1sc), 1sc into next and each ch to end, turn.

2nd row: 3ch (count as 1dc), skip 1 st, *2CC over next 2 sts, 1dc into each of next 6 sts, rep from * to last 3 sts, 2CC over next 2 sts, 1dc into tch, turn.

3rd row: 1ch (counts as 1sc), skip 1 st, 1sc into next and each st to end, working last st into top of tch, turn.

4th row: 3ch (counts as 1dc), skip 1 st, 1dc into each of next 4 sts, *2CC over next 2 sts, 1dc into each of next 6 sts; rep from * to last 7 sts, 2CC over next 2 sts, 1dc into each of last 5 sts, working last st into tch, turn.

5th row: As 3rd row.

Rep 2nd to 5th rows.

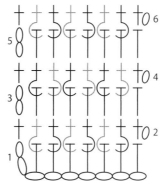

Crinkle Stitch I

Multiple of 2 sts.

(add 1 for base chain)

Special Abbreviation: Sc/rf (raised single crochet at the front of the fabric) = Wrap the yarn around the hook, insert the hook from in front and from right to left around the stem of the appropriate stitch, and complete the stitch normally.

Sc/rb (raised single crochet at the back of the fabric) = Wrap the yarn around the hook, insert the hook from behind and from right to left around the stem of the appropriate stitch, and complete the stitch normally.

1st row (wrong side): Skip 2ch (count as 1hdc), 1hdc into each ch to end, turn.

2nd row: 1ch, 1sc into first st, *1sc/rf around next st, 1sc/rb around next st; rep from * ending 1sc into top of tch, turn.

3rd row: 2ch (count as 1hdc), skip first st, 1hdc into next and each st to end, skip tch, turn.

4th row: 1ch, 1sc into first st, *1sc/rb around next st, 1sc/rf around next st; rep from * ending 1sc into top of tch, turn.

5th row: As 3rd row.

Rep 2nd to 5th rows.

Crinkle Stitch II

Work as Crinkle Stitch I (page 147), but using wrong side of fabric as the right side.

Accessories are great first projects for experimenting with crochet and trying out the stitches in this book! Bags that can be made as simple oblongs and folded as clutch bags or fastened to a handle are ideal starter projects.

Boxed Block Stitch

Work as Boxed Shell Stitch (page 39), except that on 2nd and every alternate row 5dc are worked under 3ch arch instead of into the actual st, thus making a block rather than a shell.

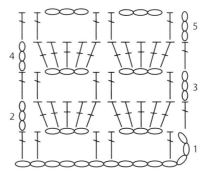

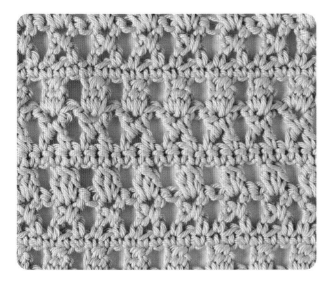

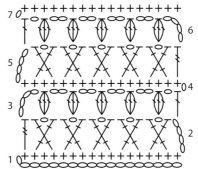

Hotcross Bun Stitch

Multiple of 3 sts + 2.

(add 1 for base chain)

Special Abbreviation: TrX (treble "X" shape – worked over 3 sts) = [yo] twice, insert hook into next st, yo, draw loop through, yo, draw through 2 loops, skip next st, yo, insert hook into next st, yo, draw loop through, [yo, draw through 2 loops] 4 times, 1ch, yo, insert hook half way down st just made where lower "legs" join, yo, draw loop through, [yo, draw through 2 loops] twice.

1st row (wrong side): 1sc into 2nd ch from hook, 1sc into next and each ch to end, turn.

2nd row: 4ch (count as 1tr), skip first st, *TrX over next 3 sts; rep from * ending 1tr into last st, skip tch, turn.

3rd row: 4ch (count as 1dc and 1ch), *work dc3tog into next 1ch sp**, 2ch; rep from * ending last rep at **, 1ch, 1dc into top of tch, turn.

4th row: 1ch, 1sc into first st, 1sc into next ch, *1sc into next cluster, 1sc into each of next 2ch; rep from * to end, turn.

Rep 2nd to 4th rows.

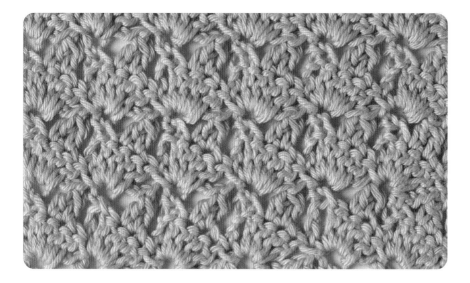

Diagonal Shell Stitch

Multiple of 4 sts + 1.

(add 1 for base chain)

Special Abbreviation: Shell = [1sc, 3ch, 4dc] all into same st.

1st row (right side): Work 1 shell into 2nd ch from hook, *skip 3ch, 1 shell into next ch; rep from * to last 4ch, skip 3ch, 1sc into last ch, turn.

2nd row: 3ch (count as 1dc), skip 1 st, *skip 1dc, over next 2 sts work dc2tog, 3ch, skip 1dc, 1sc into top of 3ch; rep from * to end, turn.

3rd row: 1ch, 1 shell into first st, *skip 3ch and next st, 1 shell into next sc; rep from * ending skip 3ch and next st, 1sc into top of tch, turn.

Rep 2nd and 3rd rows.

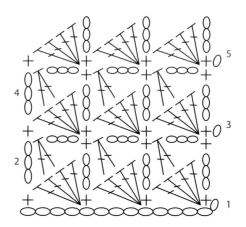

Singles and Doubles

Any number of sts.

(add 1 for base chain)

1st row (wrong side): Skip 2ch (count as 1sc), 1sc into next and each ch to end, turn.

2nd row: 3ch (counts as 1dc), skip 1 st, 1dc into next and each st to end, working last st into top of tch, turn.

3rd row: 1ch (counts as 1sc), skip 1 st, 1sc into next and each st to end, working last st into top of tch, turn.

Rep 2nd and 3rd rows.

Note: This is one of the simplest and most effective combination stitch patterns. It is also one of the easiest to get wrong! Concentration is required as you work the ends of the rows to avoid increasing or decreasing, or working two rows of the same stitch in succession by mistake.

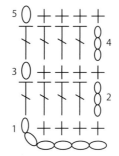

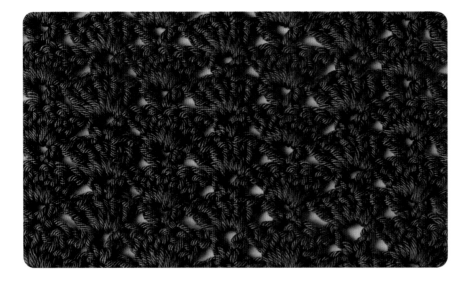

Shell and V Stitch

Multiple of 8 sts + 1.

(add 2 for base chain)

1st row (right side): Skip 2ch (count as 1dc), 2dc into next ch, *skip 3ch, work a V st of [1dc, 1ch, 1dc] into next ch, skip 3ch**, 5dc into next ch; rep from * ending last rep at **, 3dc into last ch, turn.

2nd row: 3ch (count as 1dc), 1dc into first st, *5dc into sp at center of next V st **, V st into 3rd of next 5dc; rep from * ending last rep at **, 2dc into top of tch, turn.

3rd row: 3ch (count as 1dc), 2dc into first st, *V st into 3rd of next 5 dc**, 5dc into sp at center of next V st; rep from * ending last rep at **, 3dc into top of tch, turn.

Rep 2nd and 3rd rows.

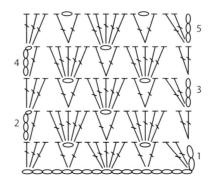

Tread Pattern

Multiple of 8 sts + 3.

(add 2 for base chain)

1st row (right side): Skip 3ch (count as 1dc), 1dc into each of next 2ch, *skip 2ch, 1dc into next ch, 3ch, work a block of 3dc evenly spaced into side of dc just made, skip 2ch, 1dc into each of next 3ch; rep from * to end, turn.

2nd row: 3ch (count as 1dc), skip first st, 1dc into each of next 2dc, *2ch, 1sc into top of 3ch at corner of next block, 2ch, skip dc that forms base of same block, 1dc into each of next 3dc; rep from * ending last rep in top of tch, turn.

3rd row: 3ch (count as 1dc), skip first st, 1dc into each of next 2dc, *skip 2ch, 1dc into next sc, 3ch, 3dc evenly spaced into side of dc just made, skip 2ch, 1dc into each of next 3dc; rep from * ending last rep in top of tch, turn. Rep 2nd and 3rd rows.

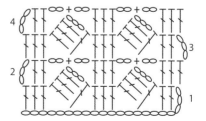

Crossed Ripple Stitch

Multiple of 3 sts + 2.

(add 1 for base chain)

Special Abbreviation: Dc/rf (raised double crochet at the front of the fabric) = Wrap the yarn around the hook, insert the hook from in front and from right to left around the stem of the appropriate stitch, and complete the stitch normally.

1st base row (wrong side): 1sc into 2nd ch from hook, 1sc into each ch to end, turn.

2nd base row: 3ch (count as 1dc), skip first st, *skip next 2 sts, 1dc into next st, 1ch, 1dc back into first of 2 sts just skipped – called Crossed Pair; rep from * ending 1dc into last st, skip tch, turn.

Commence Pattern

1st row: 1ch, 1sc into first st, 1sc into next and each st and each ch sp to end, working last st into top of tch, turn.

2nd row: As 2nd base row, except as 2nd st of each Crossed Pair work 1dc/rf loosely around first st of corresponding Crossed Pair 2 rows below.

Rep these 2 rows.

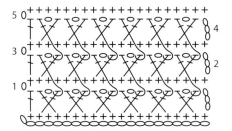

Track Stitch

Any number of sts.

(add 1 for base chain)

1st row (wrong side): Skip 2ch (count as 1sc), 1sc into next and each ch to end, turn.

2nd row: 5ch (count as 1dtr), skip 1 st, 1dtr into next and each st to end, working last st into top of tch, turn.

3rd, 4th, and 5th rows: 1ch (counts as 1sc), skip 1 st, 1sc into next and each st to end, working last st into top of tch, turn.

Rep 2nd to 5th rows.

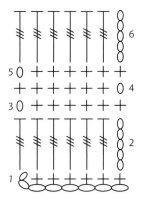

Sidesaddle Shell Stitch

Multiple of 6 sts + 1.

(add 3 for base chain)

Special Abbreviation: Shell = 3dc, 1ch, [1sc, 1hdc, 1dc] all into side of last of 3dc just made.

1st row (wrong side): Skip 3ch (count as 1dc), 3dc into next ch, skip 2ch, 1sc into next ch, *skip 2ch, Shell into next ch, skip 2ch, 1sc into next ch; rep from * to last 3ch, skip 2ch, 4dc into last ch, turn.

2nd row: 1ch (counts as 1sc), skip 1 st, *skip next 3 sts, Shell into next sc, skip 3 sts, 1sc into next ch sp; rep from * ending last rep with 1sc into top of tch, turn.

3rd row: 3ch (count as 1dc), 3dc into first st, skip 3 sts, 1sc into next ch sp, *skip 3 sts, Shell into next sc, skip 3 sts, 1sc into next ch sp; rep from * ending skip 3 sts, 4dc into tch, turn.

Rep 2nd and 3rd rows.

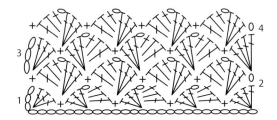

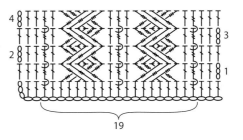

Gwenyth's Cable

Worked over 19 sts on a background of basic double crochets with any number of sts.

Special Abbreviation: Tr/rf (raised treble crochet at the front of the fabric) = Wrap the yarn around the hook, insert the hook from in front and from right to left around the stem of the appropriate stitch, and complete the stitch normally.

Tr/rb (raised treble crochet at the back of the fabric) = Wrap the yarn around the hook, insert the hook from behind and from right to left around the stem of the appropriate stitch, and complete the stitch normally.

1st row (right side): 1tr/rf around first st, 1dc into next st, skip next 3 sts, 1dtr into each of next 3 sts, going behind last 3dtrs work 1dtr into each of 3 sts just skipped, 1dc into next st, 1tr/rf around next st, 1dc into next st, skip next 3 sts, 1dtr into each of next 3 sts, going in front of last 3dtrs but not catching them work 1dtr into each of 3 sts just skipped, 1dc into next st, 1tr/rf around next st.

2nd row: As 1st row, except work 1tr/rb instead of rf over first, 10th and 19th sts to keep raised ridges on right side of fabric.

Rep 1st and 2nd rows.

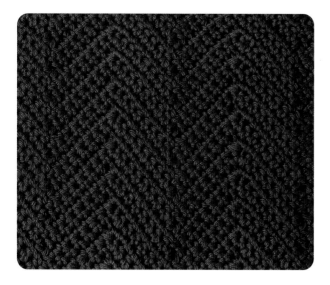

Chevron Stitch I

Multiple of 16 sts + 2.

1st row (right side): Work 2sc into 2nd ch from hook, *1sc into each of next 7ch, skip 1ch, 1sc into each of next 7ch, 3sc into next ch; rep from * to end omitting 1sc at end of last rep, turn.

2nd row: 1ch, work 2sc into first sc, *1sc into each of next 7sc, skip 2sc, 1sc into each of next 7sc, 3sc into next sc; rep from * to end, omitting 1sc at end of last rep, turn.
Rep 2nd row only.

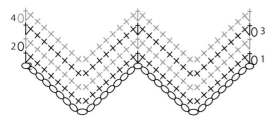

Chevron Stitch II

Work as given for Chevron Stitch I (this page), working 1 row each in colors A, B, and C throughout.

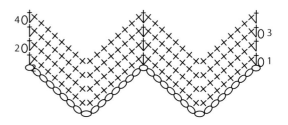

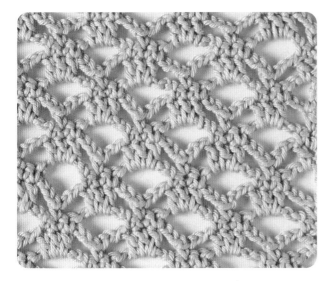

Arched Lace Stitch

Multiple of 8 sts + 1.

(add 1 for base chain)

1st row (right side): 1sc into 2nd ch from hook, 1sc into next ch, *5ch, skip 5ch, 1sc into each of next 3ch; rep from * omitting 1sc at end of last rep, turn.

2nd row: 1ch, 1sc into first st, *3ch, skip next sc, 3dc into next 5ch arch, 3ch, skip 1sc, 1sc into next sc; rep from * to end, skip tch, turn.

3rd row: 6ch (count as 1tr and 2ch), skip 3ch, *1sc into each of next 3dc**, 5ch, skip [3ch, 1sc and 3ch]; rep from * ending last rep at **, 2ch, skip 3ch, 1tr into last sc, skip tch, turn.

4th row: 3ch (count as 1dc), skip first st, 1dc into 2ch sp, *3ch, skip next sc, 1sc into next sc, 3ch, skip 1sc**, 3dc into next 5ch arch; rep from * ending last rep at **, skip 1ch, 1dc into each of next 2ch of tch, turn.

5th row: 1ch, 1sc into first st, 1sc into next st, *5ch, skip [3ch, 1sc and 3ch], 1sc into each of next 3dc; rep from * to end, omitting 1sc at end of last rep, turn.

Rep 2nd to 5th rows.

Interlocking Block Stitch 1

Multiple of 6 sts + 3.

(add 2 for base chain)

Special Abbreviation: Sdc (Spike double crochet) = work dc over ch sp by inserting hook into top of next row below (or base chain).

Work 1 row each in colors A, B, and C throughout.

1st row: Skip 3ch (count as 1dc), 1dc into each of next 2ch, *3ch, skip 3ch, 1dc into each of next 3ch; rep from * to end, turn.

2nd row: *3ch, skip 3 sts, 1Sdc over each of next 3 sts; rep from * to last 3 sts, 2ch, skip 2 sts, sl st into top of tch, turn.

3rd row: 3ch (count as 1Sdc), skip 1 st, 1Sdc over each of next 2 sts, *3ch, skip 3 sts, 1Sdc over each of next 3 sts; rep from * to end, turn.

Rep 2nd and 3rd rows.

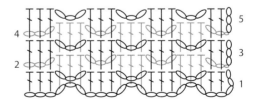

Interlocking Block Stitch II

Work as Interlocking Block Stitch I (page 160).
Work 1 row each in colors A and B alternately
throughout. Do not break yarn when changing color,
but begin row at same end as color.

When using two different colors in the same row always
work over the color not in use. When changing color, draw
the new color through all the loops on the hook of the last
stitch in the previous color.

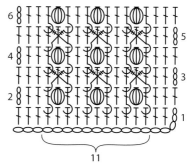

Crossed Puff Cables

Worked over 11 sts on a background of basic double crochets with any number of sts.

Special Abbreviation: Tr/rf (raised treble crochet at the front of the fabric) = Wrap the yarn around the hook, insert the hook from in front and from right to left around the stem of the appropriate stitch, and complete the stitch normally.

Tr/rb (raised treble crochet at the back of the fabric) = Wrap the yarn around the hook, insert the hook from behind and from right to left around the stem of the appropriate stitch, and complete the stitch normally.

1st row (right side): 1dc into each st.

2nd row: *1tr/rb around next st, work a Puff st of

hdc5tog all into next st, 1tr/rb around next st**, 1dc into next st; rep from * once and from * to ** again.

3rd row: *Leaving last loop of each st on hook work [1dc into next st, skip Puff st, work 1tr/rf around next st] ending yo, draw through all 3 loops on hook, 1dc into top of Puff st, leaving last loop of each st on hook work [1tr/rf around st before same Puff st and 1dc into top of st after Puff st] ending yo, draw through all 3 loops on hook**, 1dc into next st; rep from * once and from * to ** again.

4th row: As 2nd row, but make new tr/rbs by inserting hook under raised stems only of previous sts.

Rep 3rd and 4th rows.

Peacock Fan Stitch

Multiple of 12 sts + 1.

(add 1 for base chain)

1st row (right side): 1sc into 2nd ch from hook, *skip 5ch, 13dtr into next ch, skip 5ch, 1sc into next ch; rep from * to end, turn.

2nd row: 5ch (count as 1dtr), 1dtr into first st, *4ch, skip 6dtr, 1sc into next dtr, 4ch, skip 6dtr**, work [1dtr, 1ch, 1dtr] into next sc; rep from * ending last rep at **, 2dtr into last sc, skip tch, turn.

3rd row: 1ch, 1sc into first st, *skip [1dtr and 4ch], 13dtr into next sc, skip [4ch and 1dtr], 1sc into next ch; rep from * to end, turn.

Rep 2nd and 3rd rows.

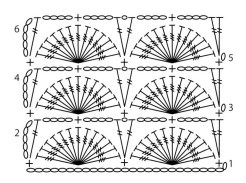

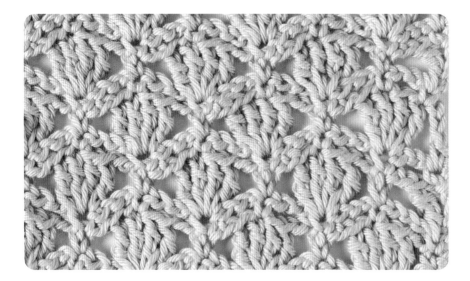

Petal Stitch

Multiple of 8 sts + 1.

(add 1 for base chain)

1st row (wrong side): 1sc into 2nd ch from hook, *2ch, skip 3ch, 4tr into next ch, 2ch, skip 3ch, 1sc into next ch; rep from * to end, turn.

2nd row: 1ch, 1sc into first st, *3ch, skip 2ch and 1tr, 1sc into next tr, 3ch, skip 2tr and 2ch, 1sc into next sc; rep from * to end, skip tch, turn.

3rd row: 4ch (count as 1tr), 1tr into first st, *2ch, skip 3ch, 1sc into next sc, 2ch, skip 3ch, 4tr into next sc; rep from * to end omitting 1tr at end of last rep, skip tch, turn.

4th row: 1ch, 1sc into first st, *3ch, skip 2tr and 2ch, 1sc into next sc, 3ch, skip 2ch and 1tr, 1sc into next tr; rep from * ending last rep in top of tch, turn.

5th row: 1ch, 1sc into first st, *2ch, skip 3ch, 4tr into next sc, 2ch, skip 3ch, 1sc into next sc; rep from * to end, skip tch, turn.

Rep 2nd to 5th rows.

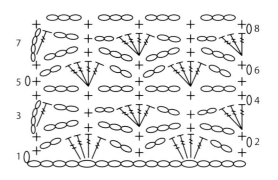

Odd Forked Cluster Stitch

Any number of sts.

(add 2 for base chain)

Special Abbreviation: OFC (Odd Forked Cluster) = yo, insert hook into ch or st as indicated, yo, draw loop through, yo, draw through 2 loops, insert hook into next ch or st, yo, draw loop through, yo, draw through all 3 loops on hook.

1st row: Skip 2ch (count as 1hdc), 1OFC inserting hook first into 3rd then 4th ch from hook, *1OFC inserting hook first into same ch as previous OFC then into next ch; rep from * until 1ch remains, 1hdc into last ch, turn.

2nd row: 2ch (count as 1hdc), 1OFC inserting hook into first st then into next st, *1OFC inserting hook into same st as previous OFC then into next st; rep from * ending 1hdc into top of tch, turn.

Rep 2nd row.

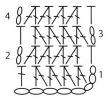

T   OFC

Diagonal Spike Stitch

Multiple of 4 sts + 2.

(add 2 for base chain)

Special Abbreviation: Sdc (Spike double crochet) = yo, insert hook into same place that first dc of previous 3dc block was worked, yo, draw loop through and up so as not to crush 3dc block, [yo, draw through 2 loops] twice.

1st row: Skip 3ch (count as 1dc), *1dc into each of next 3ch, skip next ch and work 1Sdc over it instead; rep from * ending 1dc into last ch, turn.

2nd row: 3ch (count as 1dc), skip 1 st, *1dc into each of next 3 sts, skip next st and work 1Sdc over it instead; rep from * ending 1dc into top of tch, turn.

Rep 2nd row.

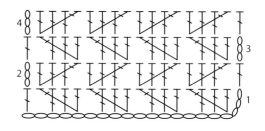

Create a simple shrug by working a shallow oblong shape, approximately 24 x 16 in. (60 x 40 cm). Lay it out flat, fold the top and bottom to the center in turn, and instead of sewing, simply fasten each seam with a decorative ribbon either side, put it on and tie in a bow!

Puff Stitch Plaits

Multiple of 8 sts + 1.

(add 1 for base chain)

1st row (right side): Skip 2ch (count as 1hdc), 1hdc into each of next 2ch, *1ch, skip 1ch, hdc3tog all into next ch, 1ch, skip 1ch**, 1hdc into each of next 5ch; rep from * ending last rep at ** when 3ch remain, 1hdc into each of last 3ch, turn.

2nd row: 2ch (count as 1hdc), skip first st, 1hdc into each of next 2 sts, *hdc3tog into next ch sp, 1ch, skip 1 st, hdc3tog into next ch sp**, 1hdc into each of next 5 sts; rep from * ending last rep at ** when 3 sts remain including tch, 1hdc into each of last 3 sts, turn.

3rd row: 2ch (count as 1hdc), skip first st, 1hdc into each of next 2 sts, *1ch, skip 1 st, hdc3tog into next ch sp, 1ch, skip 1 st**, 1hdc into each of next 5 sts; rep from * ending last rep at ** when 3 sts remain including tch, 1hdc into each of last 3 sts, turn.

Rep 2nd and 3rd rows.

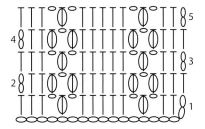

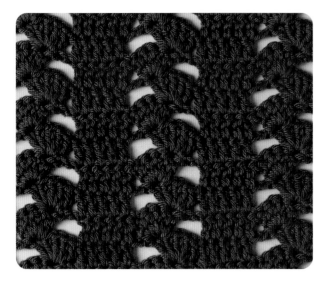

Block and Offset Shell Stitch

Multiple of 11 sts + 5.

(add 2 for base chain)

1st row (right side): Skip 3ch (count as 1dc), 1dc into each of next 4ch, *skip 2ch, 5dc into next ch, 2ch, skip 3ch, 1dc into each of next 5ch; rep from * to end, turn.

2nd row: 3ch (count as 1dc), skip first st, 1dc into each of next 4 sts, *skip 2ch, 5dc into next dc, 2ch, skip 4dc, 1dc into each of next 5 sts; rep from * to end, turn.

Rep 2nd row.

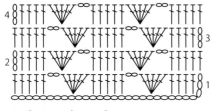

Aligned Cobble Stitch

Multiple of 2 sts + 1.

(add 1 for base chain)

1st row (right side): 1sc into 2nd ch from hook, 1sc into each ch to end, turn.

2nd row: 1ch, 1sc into first st, *1tr into next st, 1sc into next st; rep from * to end, skip tch, turn.

3rd row: 1ch, 1sc into first st, 1sc into next and each st to end, skip tch, turn.

Rep 2nd and 3rd rows.

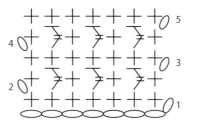

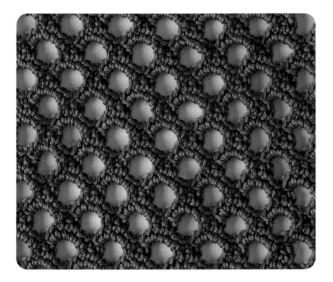

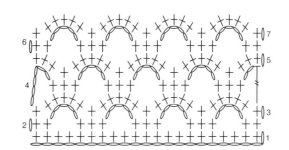

Honeycomb Trellis

Multiple of 5 sts + 2.

1st row (right side): Work 1sc into 2nd ch from hook, 1sc into each ch to end, turn.

2nd row: 1ch, 1sc into each of first 2sc, *5ch, skip 2sc, 1sc into each of next 3sc; rep from * to end omitting 1sc at end of last rep, turn.

3rd row: 1ch, 1sc into first sc, *5sc into next 5ch arch, skip 1sc, 1sc into next sc; rep from * to end, turn.

4th row: 6ch (count as 1tr, 2ch), skip first 2sc, 1sc into each of next 3sc, *5ch, skip 3sc, 1sc into each of next 3sc; rep from * to last 2sc, 2ch, 1tr into last sc, turn.

5th row: 1ch, 1sc into first tr, 2sc into 2ch sp, skip 1sc, 1sc into next sc, *5sc into next 5ch arch, skip 1sc, 1sc into next sc; rep from * to last 2ch sp, 2sc into last sp, 1sc into 4th of 6ch at beg of previous row, turn.

6th row: 1ch, 1sc into each of first 2sc, *5ch, skip 3sc, 1sc into each of next 3sc; rep from * to end omitting 1sc at end of last rep, turn.

Rep 3rd to 6th rows.

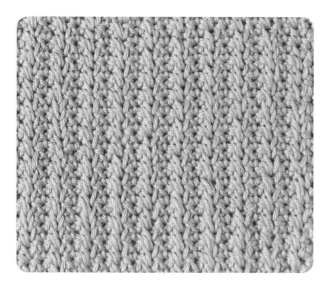

Alternating Spike Stitch I

Multiple of 2 sts.

(add 1 for base chain)

Special Abbreviation: Ssc (Spike single crochet) = insert hook below next st 1 row down (i.e. into same place as that st was worked), yo, draw loop through and up to height of present row, yo, draw through both loops on hook.

1st row: Skip 2ch (count as 1sc), 1sc into next and each ch to end, turn.

2nd row: 1ch (counts as 1sc), skip 1 st, *1sc into next st, 1Ssc over next st; rep from * ending 1sc into tch, turn.

Rep 2nd row.

Alternating Spike Stitch II

Work as Alternating Spike Stitch I (this page).

Work 1 row each in colors A, B, and C throughout.

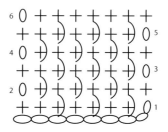

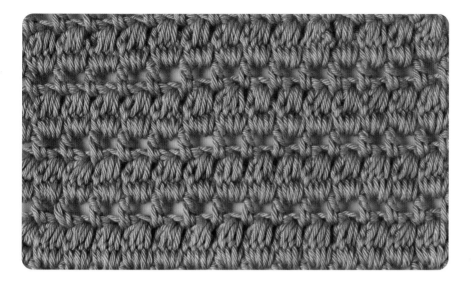

Aligned Puff Stitch

Multiple of 2 sts + 1.

(add 1 for base chain)

1st row (right side): 1sc into 2nd ch from hook, *1ch, skip 1ch, 1sc into next ch; rep from * to end, turn.

2nd row: 2ch (count as 1hdc), skip first st, *hdc4tog all into next ch sp, 1ch, skip 1sc; rep from * ending hdc4tog into last ch sp, 1hdc into last sc, skip tch, turn.

3rd row: 1ch, 1sc into first st, *1ch, skip 1 st, 1sc into next ch sp; rep from * ending in top of tch, turn.

Rep 2nd and 3rd rows.

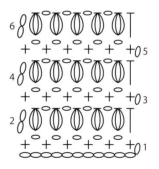

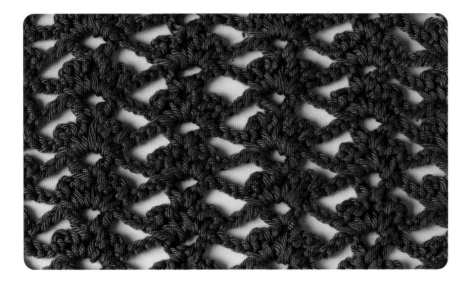

Triple Picot V Stitch

Multiple of 11 sts + 7.

(add 3 for base chain)

1st row (right side): 1dc into 4th ch from hook, *3ch, skip 3ch, 1sc into next ch**, work a picot of [3ch, 1sc into next ch] 3 times, 3ch, skip 3ch, [1dc, 2ch, 1dc] into next ch; rep from * ending last rep at ** when 2ch remain, 3ch, 1sc into next ch, 1ch, 1hdc into last ch, turn.

2nd row: 4ch (count as 1dc and 1ch), 1dc into first st, *3ch, skip 1 Picot and 3ch**, into next 2ch sp work 1sc, [3ch, 1sc] 3 times, then 3ch, skip 3ch and 1 Picot, [1dc, 2ch, 1dc] into next Picot; rep from * ending last rep at **, work [1sc, 3ch, 1sc] into top of tch, 1ch, 1hdc into next ch, turn.

Rep 2nd row.

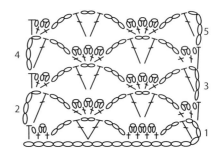

Broomstick Lace

Multiple of 4 sts.

(add 1 for base chain)

1st row (right side): 1sc into 2nd ch from hook, 1sc into next and each ch to end, turn.

2nd row: 1ch, 1sc into first st, 1sc into next and each st to end, skip tch, turn.

3rd row: *1ch, draw loop on hook up to approx height of dtr; keeping loop on hook and not allowing it to change size through yarn slippage, insert hook into next st, yo, draw loop through; rep from * to end, keeping all lace loops on hook. At end remove all except last lace loop from hook, yo, draw loop through, turn.

4th row: *Always inserting hook through next 4 lace loops together work 4sc; rep from * to end, turn.

Rep 2nd to 4th rows.

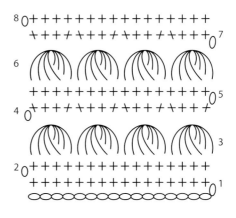

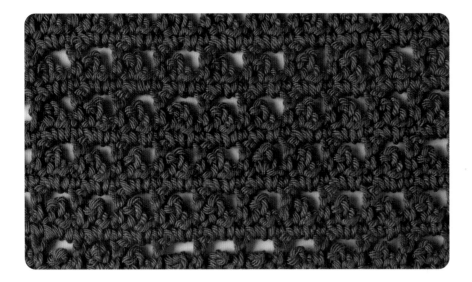

Arch Gallery

Multiple of 3 sts + 2.

1st row (right side): Work 1sc into 2nd ch from hook, 1sc into next ch, *4ch, sl st into 4th ch from hook (1 picot made), 1sc into each of next 3ch; rep from * to end omitting 1sc at end of last rep, turn.

2nd row: 5ch (count as 1dc, 2ch), skip 2sc, 1dc into next sc, *2ch, skip 2sc, 1dc into next sc; rep from * to end, turn.

3rd row: 1ch, 1sc into first dc, *into next 2ch sp work [1sc, 1picot, 1sc], 1sc into next dc; rep from * to end placing last sc into 3rd of 5ch at beg of previous row, turn. Rep 2nd and 3rd rows.

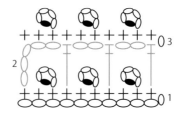

Boxed Puff Stitch

Multiple of 3 sts + 1.

(add 4 for base chain)

Special Abbreviation: Puff Stitch = hdc4tog all into same st and closed with 1ch drawn tightly.

1st row (right side): Puff st into 5th ch from hook, *skip 2ch, [1dc, 2ch, puff st] all into next ch; rep from * ending skip 2ch, 1dc into last ch, turn.

2nd row: 1ch, skip first st, *work 1dc loosely over next row into first of 2 skipped sts in row below, 1sc into puff st, 1sc into next 2ch sp; rep from * ending 1sc into 3rd ch of tch, turn.

3rd row: 5ch (count as 1dc and 2ch), puff st into first st, *skip 2sc, [1dc, 2ch, puff st] all into next dc; rep from * ending skip 2sc, 1dc into last dc, skip tch, turn.

Rep 2nd and 3rd rows.

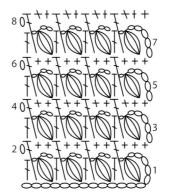

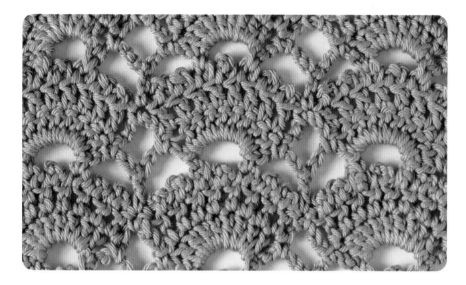

Picot Fan Stitch

Multiple of 12 sts + 1.

(add 1 for base chain)

1st row (right side): 1sc into 2nd ch from hook, *5ch, skip 3ch, 1sc into next ch; rep from * to end, turn.

2nd row: 5ch (count as 1dc and 2ch), *1sc into next 5ch arch, 8dc into next arch, 1sc into next arch**, 5ch; rep from * ending last rep at ** in last arch, 2ch, 1dc into last sc, skip tch, turn.

3rd row: 1ch, 1sc into first st, skip 2ch and 1sc, *work a picot of [1dc into next dc, 3ch, insert hook down through top of dc just made and sl st to close] 7 times, 1dc into next dc, 1sc into next arch; rep from * to end, turn.

4th row: 8ch, skip 2 picots, *1sc into next picot, 5ch, skip 1 picot, 1sc into next picot, 5ch, skip 2 picots, 1dc into next sc**, 5ch, skip 2 picots; rep from * ending last rep at **, skip tch, turn.

5th row: 5ch (count as 1dc and 2ch), *1sc into next 5ch arch, 8dc into next arch, 1sc into next arch**, 5ch; rep from * ending last rep at ** in last arch, 2ch, 1dc into 3rd ch of tch, turn.

Rep 3rd to 5th rows.

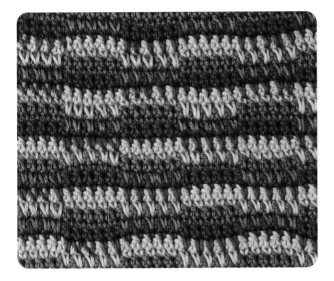

Spiked Squares

Multiple of 10 sts + 2.

(add 1 for base chain)

Special Abbreviation: Ssc (Spike single crochet) work as in Arrowhead Spike Stitch (page 169).

Note: when working Sscs over previous Sscs, be careful to insert hook in centers of previous Sscs.

Work 2 rows each in colors A, B, and C throughout.

Base row (right side): 1sc into 2nd ch from hook, 1sc into next and each ch to end, turn.

Commence Pattern

1st row: 1ch, 1sc into first and each st to end, skip tch, turn.

2nd row: 1ch, 1sc into first st, *1Ssc2 over each of next 5 sts, 1sc into each of next 5 sts; rep from * ending 1sc into last sc, skip tch, turn.

Rep the last 2 rows 3 times more.

9th row: As 1st row.

10th row: 1ch, 1sc into first st, *1sc into each of next 5 sts, 1Ssc2 over each of next 5 sts; rep from * ending 1sc into last sc, skip tch, turn.

Rep the last 2 rows 3 times more.

Rep these 16 rows.

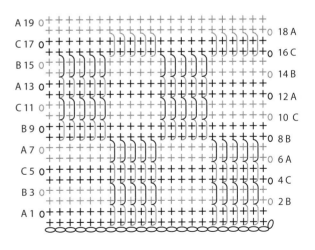

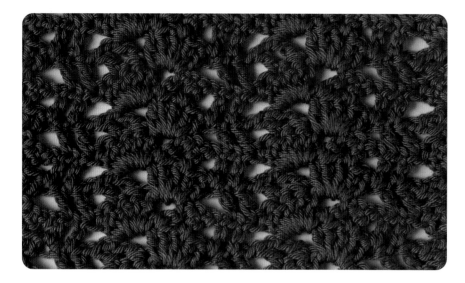

Lacy Wave Stitch

Multiple of 11 sts + 1.

(add 1 for base chain)

1st row (right side): 1sc into 2nd ch from hook, *2ch, skip 2ch, 1dc into each of next 2ch, 2ch, skip 2ch, 1sc into each of next 5ch; rep from * to end, turn.

2nd row: 5ch (count as 1dc and 2ch), 1dc into first st, *[1ch, skip 1 st, 1dc into next st] twice, 1ch, 1dc into next 2ch sp, skip 2dc**, 5dc into next 2ch sp, 2ch, 1dc into next st; rep from * ending last rep at **, 4dc into last 2ch sp, 1dc into last sc, skip tch, turn.

3rd row: 5ch (count as 1dc and 2ch), 1dc into first st, *[1ch, skip 1 st, 1dc into next st] twice, 1ch, skip 1 st, 1dc into next ch, skip [1dc, 1ch, 1dc, 1ch and 1dc], 5dc into next 2ch sp**, 2ch, 1dc into next st; rep from * ending last rep at ** in tch, turn.

Rep 3rd row.

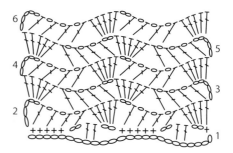

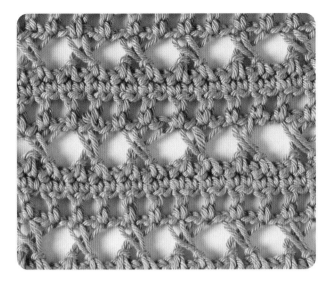

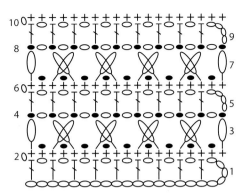

Crossed Lace Loop Stitch

Multiple of 4 sts + 3.

(add 3 for base chain)

1st row (right side): 1dc into 6th ch from hook, *1ch, skip 1ch, 1dc into next ch; rep from * to end, turn.

2nd row: 1ch, 1sc into first st, *1sc into next ch, 1sc into next dc; rep from * ending 1sc into each of next 2ch of tch, turn.

3rd row: *1ch, draw loop on hook up to approx height of tr; keeping loop on hook and not allowing it to change size through yarn slippage, insert hook into next st, yo, draw loop through, sl st into next st; rep from * to end, keeping all lace loops on hook. At end remove all except

last lace loop from hook, yo, draw loop through, insert hook under back thread as though for Solomon's Knot (page 233), but make sl st to lock last lace loop, turn.

4th row: Skip first lace loop, *ch1, skip 1 lace loop, sl st into top of next loop, 1ch, bring forward loop just skipped and sl st into top of it; rep from * ending ch1, sl st into top of last loop, turn.

5th row: 4ch (count as 1dc and 1ch), skip 1ch, 1dc into next sl st, *1ch, skip 1ch, 1dc into next sl st; rep from * to end, turn.

Rep 2nd to 5th rows.

Grit Stitch I

Multiple of 2 sts + 1.

(add 2 for base chain)

1st row: Skip 2ch (count as 1sc), 1sc into next ch, *skip 1ch, 2sc into next ch; rep from * to last 2ch, skip 1ch, 1sc into last ch, turn.

2nd row: 1ch (counts as 1sc), 1sc into first st, *skip 1sc, 2sc into next sc; rep from * to last 2 sts, skip 1sc, 1sc into top of tch, turn.

Rep 2nd row.

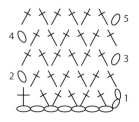

Grit Stitch II

Multiple of 2 sts + 1.

(add 2 for base chain)

1st row: Skip 2ch (count as 1sc), 1dc into next ch, *skip 1ch, work [1sc and 1dc] into next ch; rep from * to last 2ch, skip 1ch, 1sc into last ch, turn.

2nd row: 1ch (counts as 1sc), 1dc into first st, *skip 1dc, work [1sc and 1dc] into next sc; rep from * to last 2 sts, skip 1dc, 1sc into top of tch, turn.

Rep 2nd row.

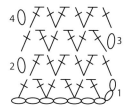

Spike Cluster Stitch

Multiple of 8 sts + 5.

(add 1 for base chain)

Special Abbreviation: SPC (Spike Cluster) = over next st pick up 5 spike loops by inserting hook as follows: 2 sts to right of next st and 1 row down; 1 st to right and 2 rows down; directly below and 3 rows down; 1 st to left and 2 rows down; 2 sts to left and 1 row down (6 loops on hook); now insert hook into top of next st itself, yo, draw loop through, yo, draw through all 7 loops on hook.

Work 4 rows each in colors A and B alternately throughout.

Base row (right side): 1sc into 2nd ch from hook, 1sc into each ch to end, turn.

Commence Pattern

1st row: 1ch, 1sc into first and each st to end, skip tch, turn.

2nd and 3rd rows: As 1st row.

4th row: 1ch, 1sc into each of first 4 sts, *1SPC over next st, 1sc into each of next 7 sts (be careful not to pick up any of the spikes of the previous SPC); rep from * ending 1sc into last st, skip tch, turn.

5th, 6th, and 7th rows: As 1st row.

8th row: 1ch, 1sc into each of first 8 sts, *1SPC over next st, 1sc into each of next 7 sts; rep from * to last 5 sts, 1SPC over next st, 1sc into each of last 4 sts, skip tch, turn.

Rep these 8 rows.

ZigZag Popcorn Network

Multiple of 10 sts + 1.

(add 4 for base chain)

Note: Popcorns occur on both right- and wrong-side rows. Be sure to push them all out on the right side of the fabric as you complete them.

1st row (right side): 1sc into 9th ch from hook, 1sc into each of next 2ch, *3ch, skip 3ch, 5dc popcorn into next ch, 3ch, skip 3ch, 1sc into each of next 3ch; rep from * to last 4ch, 3ch, skip 3ch, 1dc into last ch, turn.

2nd row: 1ch, 1sc into first st, *1sc into next arch, 3ch, 5dc popcorn into 2nd of next 3sc, 3ch**, 1sc into next arch, 1sc into next popcorn; rep from * ending last rep at **, skip 2ch of tch arch, 1sc into each of next 2ch, turn.

3rd row: 6ch (count as 1dc and 3ch), *1sc into next arch, 1sc into next popcorn, 1sc into next arch, 3ch**, 5dc popcorn into 2nd of next 3sc, 3ch; rep from * ending last rep at **, 1dc into last sc, skip tch, turn.

Rep 2nd and 3rd rows.

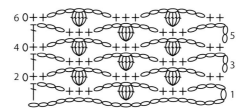

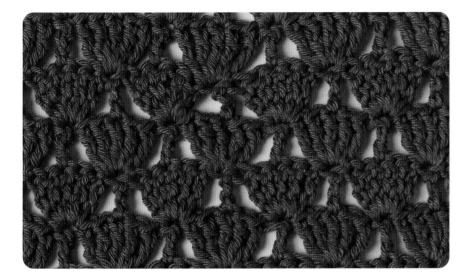

Column and Bowl

Multiple of 8 sts + 12.

1st row (right side): Work 5tr into 8th ch from hook, skip 3ch, 1tr into next ch, *skip 3ch, 5tr into next ch, skip 3ch, 1tr into next ch; rep from * to end, turn.

2nd row: 4ch (count as 1tr), 2tr into first tr, skip 2tr, 1tr into next tr, *skip 2tr, 5tr into next tr, skip 2tr, 1tr into next tr; rep from * to last 3 sts, skip 2tr, 3tr into next ch, turn.

3rd row: 4ch, skip first tr, *skip 2tr, 5tr into next tr, skip 2tr, 1tr into next tr; rep from * to end placing last tr into 4th of 4ch at beg of previous row, turn.

Rep 2nd and 3rd rows.

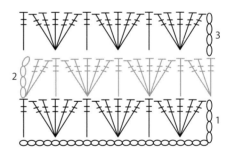

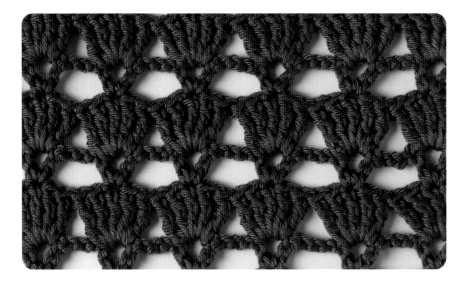

Column Stitch

Multiple of 5 sts + 6.

1st row (wrong side): Work [1dc, 2ch, 1dc] into 8th ch from hook, *3ch, skip 4ch, work [1dc, 2ch, 1dc] into next ch; rep from * to last 3ch, 2ch, 1dc into last ch, turn.

2nd row: 4ch (count as 1tr), skip first 2ch sp, work 5tr into next 2ch sp, *skip 3ch sp, work 5tr into next 2ch sp; rep from * to last sp, skip 2ch, 1tr into next ch, turn.

3rd row: 5ch (count as 1dc, 2ch), skip first 3tr, into next tr work [1dc, 2ch, 1dc], *3ch, skip 4tr, into next tr work [1dc, 2ch, 1dc]; rep from * to last 3tr, 2ch, 1dc into 4th of 4ch at beg of previous row, turn.

Rep 2nd and 3rd rows.

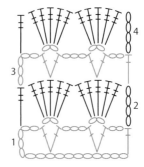

5-Star Marguerite Stitch

Multiple of 2 sts + 1.

(add 1 for base chain)

Special Abbreviation: M5C (Marguerite Cluster with 5 spike loops) = pick up spike loops (ie: yo and draw through) inserting hook as follows: into loop that closed previous M5C, under 2 threads of last spike loop of same M5C, into same place that last spike loop of same M5C was worked, into each of next 2 sts (6 loops on hook), yo, draw through all loops on hook.

1st row (wrong side): 1sc into 2nd ch from hook, 1sc into next and each ch to end, turn.

2nd row: 3ch, 1M5C inserting hook into 2nd and 3rd chs from hook and then first 3 sts to pick up 5 spike loops, *1ch, 1M5C; rep from * to end, skip tch, turn.

3rd row: 1ch, 1sc into loop that closed last M5C, *1sc into next ch, 1sc into loop that closed next M5C; rep from * ending 1sc into each of next 2ch of tch, turn.

Rep 2nd and 3rd rows.

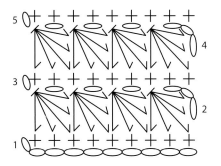

Astrakhan Stitch

Any number of sts.

(add 2 for base chain)

Note: work all rows with right side facing, i.e. work even-numbered rows from left to right.

1st row (right side): Skip 3ch (count as 1dc), 1dc into each ch to end. Do not turn.

2nd row: *7ch, sl st into front loop only of next dc to right; rep from * ending 7ch, sl st into top of tch at beginning of row. Do not turn.

3rd row: 3ch (count as 1dc), skip 1 st, 1dc into back loop only of next and each st of second-to-last row to end. Do not turn.

Rep 2nd and 3rd rows.

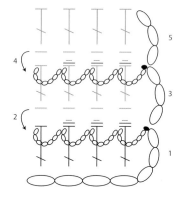

Carpet Bag Stitch

Multiple 5 sts + 6.

Special Abbreviation: Dc2tog = work 2dc into next st until 1 loop of each remains on hook, yo and through all 3 loops on hook.

1st row (right side): Work dc2tog into 6th ch from hook, (count as 1dc and 2ch sp), *skip 4ch, dc2tog into next ch, 2ch, into same ch as last dc2tog work [dc2tog, 2ch, dc2tog]; rep from * to last 5ch, skip 4ch, into last ch work [dc2tog, 2ch, 1dc], turn.

2nd row: 1ch, 1sc into first dc, *4ch, skip 2 dc2tog, 1sc into top of next dc2tog; rep from * to end placing last sc into 3rd ch, turn.

3rd row: 5ch (count as 1dc, 2ch), dc2tog into first sc, *dc2tog into next sc, 2ch, into same st as last dc2tog work [dc2tog, 2ch, dc2tog]; rep from * to last sc, into last sc work [dc2tog, 2ch, 1dc], turn.

Rep 2nd and 3rd rows.

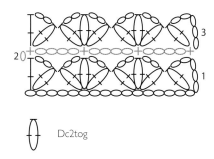

Dc2tog

Little Wave Stitch

Multiple of 4 sts + 1.

(add 1 for base chain)

Work 2 rows each in colors A and B alternately.

1st row (right side): 1sc into 2nd ch from hook, *1hdc into next ch, 1dc into next ch, 1hdc into next ch, 1sc into next ch; rep from * to end, turn.

2nd row: 1ch, 1sc into first st, *1hdc into next hdc, 1dc into next dc, 1hdc into next hdc, 1sc into next sc; rep from * to end, skip tch, turn.

3rd row: 3ch (count as 1dc), skip first st, *1hdc into next hdc, 1sc into next dc, 1hdc into next hdc, 1dc into next sc; rep from * to end, skip tch, turn.

4th row: 3ch (count as 1dc), skip first st, *1hdc into next hdc, 1sc into next sc, 1hdc into next hdc, 1dc into next dc; rep from * ending last rep in top of tch, turn.

5th row: 1ch, 1sc into first st, *1hdc into next hdc, 1dc into next sc, 1hdc into next hdc, 1sc into next dc; rep from * ending last rep in top of tch, turn.

Rep 2nd to 5th rows.

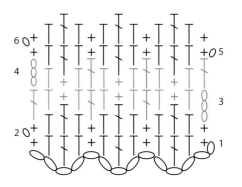

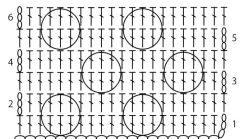

Embossed Roundels

Multiple of 8 sts + 5.

(add 2 for base chain)

Special Abbreviation: ERd (Embossed Roundel) = work [1dc, 2ch] 9 times all into same st, remove hook from working loop, insert hook from back through top of first dc of Roundel and, keeping sts of Roundel at back of fabric, pick up working loop again and draw through to close Roundel.

1st row (right side): Skip 3ch (count as 1dc), 1dc into next and each ch to end, turn.

2nd row: 3ch (count as 1dc), skip 1 st, 1dc into each of next 3 sts, *1ERd into next st, 1dc into each of next 7 sts; rep from * ending 1dc into top of tch, turn.

3rd row: 3ch (count as 1dc), skip 1 st, 1dc into next and each st to end, working last st into top of tch, turn.

4th row: 3ch (count as 1dc), skip 1 st, *1dc into each of next 7 sts, 1ERd into next st; rep from * to last 4 sts, 1dc into each of last 4 sts, turn.

5th row: As 3rd row.

Rep 2nd to 5th rows.

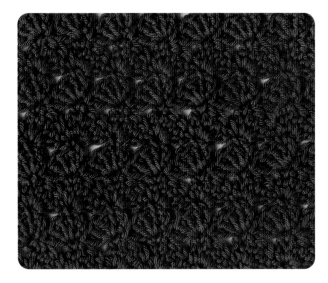

Candy Cover

Multiple of 4 sts + 4.

1st row (right side): Work 4dc into 4th ch from hook, skip 3ch, 1sc into next ch, *2ch, 4dc into same ch as last sc, skip 3ch, 1sc into next ch; rep from * to end, turn.

2nd row: 5ch, work 4dc into 4th ch from hook, *skip 4dc, 1sc between last dc skipped and next 2ch, 2ch, 4dc into side of last sc worked; rep from * to last 4dc, skip 4dc, 1sc into next ch, turn.

Rep 2nd row.

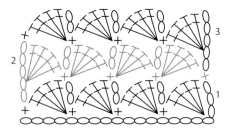

Offset Filet Network

Multiple of 2 sts.

(add 3 for base chain)

1st row (right side): 1dc into 6th ch from hook, *1ch, skip 1ch, 1dc into next ch; rep from * ending 1dc into last ch, turn.

2nd row: 4ch (count as 1dc and 1ch), skip first 2 sts, 1dc into next ch sp, *1ch, skip 1dc, 1dc into next sp; rep from * to tch, 1dc into next ch, turn.

Rep 2nd row.

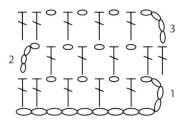

Wavy Puff Stitch Sprays

Multiple of 17 sts.

(add 2 for base chain)

1st row (right side): 1dc into 4th ch from hook (counts as dc2tog), [dc2tog over next 2ch] twice, *[1ch, work hdc4tog into next ch] 5 times, 1ch**, [dc2tog over next 2ch] 6 times; rep from * ending last rep at ** when 6ch remain, [dc2tog over next 2ch] 3 times, turn.

2nd row: 1ch, 1sc into first st and then into each st and each ch sp to end excluding tch, turn.

3rd row: 3ch, skip first st, 1dc into next st (counts as dc2tog), [dc2tog over next 2 sts] twice, *[1ch, work hdc4tog into next st] 5 times, 1ch**, [dc2tog over next 2 sts] 6 times; rep from * ending last rep at ** when 6 sts remain, [dc2tog over next 2 sts] 3 times, skip tch, turn.

Rep 2nd and 3rd rows.

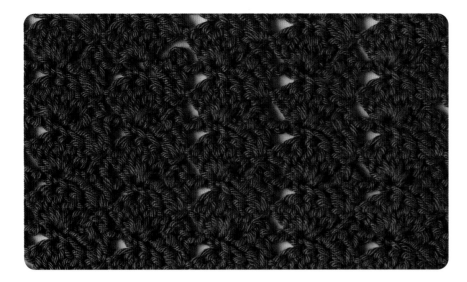

Shell Filigree Stitch

Multiple of 5 sts + 1.

(add 2 for base chain)

1st row (wrong side): 2dc into 3rd ch from hook, *1ch, skip 4ch, 5dc into next ch; rep from * working only 3dc at end of last rep, turn.

2nd row: 1ch, 1sc into first st, *2ch, skip 2dc, work a Picot V st of [1dc, 3ch, insert hook down through top of dc just made and work a sl st to close, 1dc] into next 1ch sp, 2ch, skip 2dc, 1sc into next dc; rep from * ending last rep in top of tch, turn.

3rd row: 3ch (count as 1dc), 2dc into first sc, *1ch, skip 2ch, Picot V st and 2ch, work 5dc into next sc; rep from * finishing with only 3dc at end of last rep, skip tch, turn.

Rep 2nd and 3rd rows.

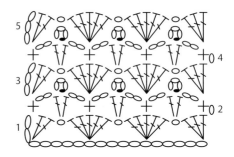

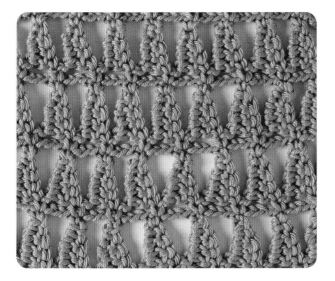

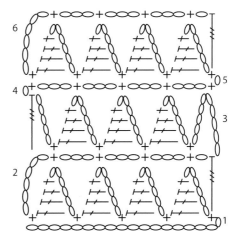

Little Pyramid Stitch

Multiple of 4 sts + 1.

(add 1 for base chain)

1st row (right side): 1sc into 2nd ch from hook, *work a Pyramid of [6ch, 1sc into 3rd ch from hook, 1dc into each of next 3ch], skip 3ch, 1sc into next ch; rep from * to end, turn.

2nd row: 6ch (count as 1dtr and 1ch), *1sc into ch at tip of next Pyramid, 3ch; rep from * ending 1sc into ch at tip of last Pyramid, 1ch, 1dtr into last sc, skip tch, turn.

3rd row: 10ch, skip 1ch, 1sc into next sc, *work Pyramid, skip 3ch, 1sc into next sc; rep from * ending 5ch, skip 1ch, 1dtr into next ch of tch, turn.

4th row: 1ch, 1sc into first st, *3ch, 1sc into ch at tip of next Pyramid; rep from * ending last rep in center of 10tch, turn.

5th row: 1ch, 1sc into first st, *work Pyramid, skip 3ch, 1sc into next sc; rep from * to end, skip tch, turn.

Rep 2nd to 5th rows.

String Network

Multiple of 4 sts + 1.

(add 5 for base chain)

1st row (right side): 1dc into 10th ch from hook, *3ch, skip 3ch, 1dc into next ch; rep from * to end, turn.

2nd row: 1ch, 1sc into first st, *3ch, skip 3ch, 1sc into next dc; rep from * ending 3ch, skip 3ch, 1sc into next ch of tch, turn.

3rd row: 6ch (count as 1dc and 3ch), skip first st and 3ch, 1dc into next sc, *3ch, skip 3ch, 1dc into next sc; rep from * to end, turn.

Rep 2nd and 3rd rows.

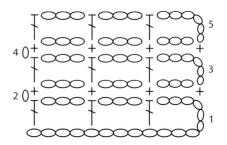

Inverted Triangles

Multiple of 6 sts + 2.

1st row (right side): Work 1sc into 2nd ch from hook, 1sc into each ch to end, turn.

2nd row: 1ch, 1sc into first sc, *6ch, work 1sc into 2nd ch from hook, then working 1 st into each of next 4ch work 1hdc, 1dc, 1tr and 1dtr; skip 5sc on previous row, 1sc into next sc; rep from * to end, turn.

3rd row: 5ch (count as 1dtr), *1sc into ch at top of next triangle, 4ch, 1dtr into next sc; rep from * to end, turn.

4th row: 1ch, work 1sc into each [dtr, ch and sc] to end, placing last sc into top of 5ch at beg of previous row, turn. Rep 2nd to 4th rows.

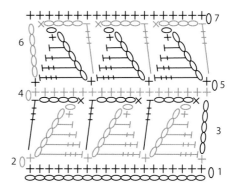

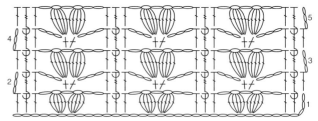

V-Twin Popcorn Stitch

Multiple of 10 sts + 3.

(add 2 for base chain)

Special Abbreviation: Tr/rf (raised treble crochet at the front of the fabric) = Wrap the yarn around the hook, insert the hook from in front and from right to left around the stem of the appropriate stitch, and complete the stitch normally.

Tr/rb (raised treble crochet at the back of the fabric) = Wrap the yarn around the hook, insert the hook from behind and from right to left around the stem of the appropriate stitch, and complete the stitch normally.

1st row (right side): Skip 3ch (count as 1dc), 1dc into each of next 2ch, *2ch, skip 3ch, 5dc popcorn into next ch, 1ch,

5dc popcorn into next ch, 1ch, skip 2ch, 1dc into each of next 3ch; rep from * to end, turn.

2nd row: 3ch (count as 1dc), skip first st, 1tr/rb around next st, 1dc into next st, *3ch, skip 1ch and 1 popcorn, 2sc into next ch sp, 3ch, skip 1 popcorn and 2ch, 1dc into next st, 1tr/rb around next st, 1dc into next st; rep from * ending last rep in top of tch, turn.

3rd row: 3ch (count as 1dc), skip first st, 1tr/rf around next st, 1dc into next st, *2ch, skip 3ch, 5dc popcorn into next sc, 1ch, 5dc popcorn into next sc, 1ch, skip 3ch, 1dc into next st, 1tr/rf around next st, 1dc into next st; rep from * ending last rep in top of tch, turn.

Rep 2nd and 3rd rows.

Shell Network

Multiple of 8 sts + 3.

(add 3 for base chain)

1st row (right side): 1dc into 6th ch from hook, *skip 2ch, 5dc into next ch, skip 2ch, 1dc into next ch, 1ch, skip 1ch, 1dc into next ch; rep from * to end, turn.

2nd row: 4ch (count as 1dc and 1ch), skip first st and next ch, 1dc into next dc, *skip 2dc, 5dc into next dc, skip 2dc, 1dc into next dc, 1ch, skip 1ch, 1dc into next dc; rep from * ending last rep in 2nd ch of tch, turn.

Rep 2nd row.

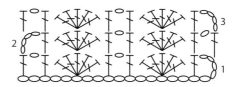

Crochet is a good choice for making clothes for new babies, as open but firm stitches allow the skin to breathe. Just take care that "holes" are not too big for little fingers to get caught.

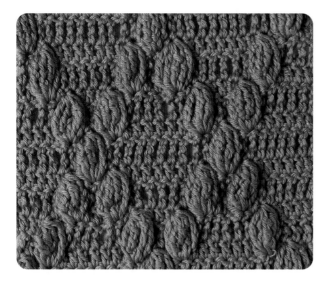

Compass Point

Multiple of 12 sts + 6.

Special Abbreviation: Bobble = working in front of work, work 5tr into ch sp 2 rows below until 1 loop of each tr remains on hook, yo and through all 6 loops.

1st row (right side): Work 1sc into 2nd ch from hook, 1sc into next ch, 1ch, skip 1ch, *1sc into each of next 11ch, 1ch, skip 1ch; rep from * to last 2ch, 1sc into each of last 2ch, turn.

2nd row: 3ch (count as 1dc), skip first sc, work 1dc into next sc, 1ch, skip 1ch sp, *1dc into each of next 11 sts, 1ch, skip 1ch sp; rep from * to last 2sc, 1dc into each of last 2sc, turn.

3rd row: 1ch, work 1sc into each of first 2dc, 1 bobble into ch sp 2 rows below, *1sc into next dc, 1ch, skip 1dc, 1sc into each of next 7dc, 1ch, skip 1dc, 1sc into next dc, 1 bobble into next ch sp 2 rows below; rep from * to last 2dc, 1sc into next dc, 1sc into 3rd of 3ch at beg of previous row, turn.

4th row: 3ch, skip first sc, 1dc into each of next 3 sts, *1ch, skip 1ch sp, 1dc into each of next 7 sts, 1ch, skip 1ch sp, 1dc into each of next 3 sts; rep from * to last sc, 1dc into last sc, turn.

5th row: 1ch, work 1sc into each of first 4dc, *1 bobble into ch sp 2 rows below, 1sc into next dc, 1ch, skip 1dc, 1sc into each of next 3dc, 1ch, skip 1dc, 1sc into next dc, 1 bobble into ch sp 2 rows below, 1sc into each of next 3dc; rep from * to last st, 1sc into 3rd of 3ch at beg of previous row, turn.

6th row: 3ch, skip first sc, work 1dc into each of next 5 sts, *1ch, skip 1ch sp, 1dc into each of next 3 sts, 1ch, skip 1ch sp, 1dc into each of next 7 sts; rep from * to end omitting 1dc at end of last rep, turn.

7th row: 1ch, work 1sc into each of first 6dc, *1 bobble into ch sp 2 rows below, 1sc into next dc, 1ch, skip 1dc, 1sc into next dc, 1 bobble into ch sp 2 rows below, 1sc into each of next 7dc; rep from * to end omitting 1sc at end of last rep, turn.

8th row: 3ch, skip first sc, work 1dc into each of next 7 sts, 1ch, skip 1ch sp, *1dc into each of next 11 sts, 1ch, skip 1ch sp; rep from * to last 8 sts, 1dc into each of last 8 sts, turn.

9th row: 1ch, work 1sc into each of first 6dc, *1ch, skip 1dc, 1sc into next dc, 1 bobble into ch sp 2 rows below, 1sc into next dc, 1ch, skip 1dc, 1sc into each of next 7dc;

rep from * to end omitting 1sc at end of last rep, turn.

10th row: As 6th row.

11th row: 1ch, work 1sc into each of first 4dc, *1ch, skip 1dc, 1sc into next dc, 1 bobble into ch sp 2 rows below, 1sc into each of next 3dc, 1 bobble into ch sp 2 rows below, 1sc into next dc, 1ch, skip 1dc, 1sc into each of next 3dc; rep from * to last dc, 1sc into 3rd of 3ch, turn.

12th row: As 4th row.

13th row: 1ch, 1sc into each of first 2dc, 1ch, skip 1dc, 1sc into next dc, *1 bobble into ch sp 2 rows below, 1sc into each of next 7dc, 1 bobble into ch sp 2 rows below, 1sc into next dc, 1ch, skip 1dc, 1sc into next dc; rep from * to last dc, 1sc into 3rd of 3ch, turn.

Rep 2nd to 13th rows.

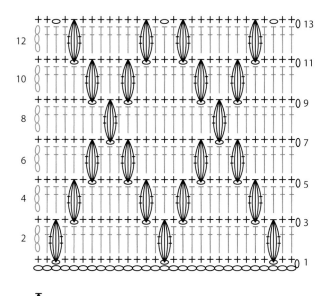

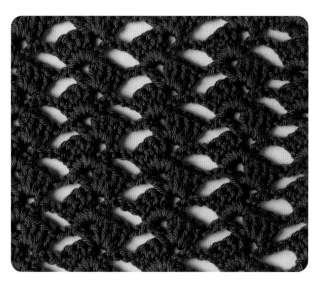

Webbed Lace Stitch

Multiple of 7 sts.

(add 4 for base chain)

1st row: 1dc into 5th ch from hook, *2ch, skip 5ch, 4dc into next ch**; 2ch, 1dc into next ch; rep from * ending last rep at ** in last ch, turn.

2nd row: 4ch, 1dc into first st, 2ch, skip [3dc, 2ch and 1dc], work [4dc, 2ch, 1dc] into next 2ch sp, *2ch, skip [4dc, 2ch and 1dc]**, work [4dc, 2ch, 1dc] into next 2ch sp; rep from * ending last rep at **, 4dc into tch, turn.

Rep 2nd row.

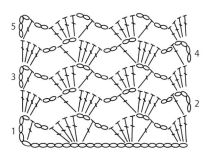

Blackberry Salad

Multiple of 4 sts + 1.

(add 2 for base chain)

1st row (right side): Skip 3ch (count as 1dc), 1dc into each ch to end, turn.

2nd row: 1ch, 1sc into each of first 2 sts, *work dc5tog into next st, 1sc into each of next 3 sts; rep from * to last 3 sts, work dc5tog into next st, 1sc into each of last 2 sts (including top of tch), turn.

3rd row: 3ch (count as 1dc), skip first st, 1dc into each st to end, skip tch, turn.

4th row: 1ch, 1sc into each of first 4 sts, *work dc5tog into next st, 1sc into each of next 3 sts; rep from * ending 1sc into top of tch, turn.

5th row: As 3rd row.

Rep 2nd to 5th rows.

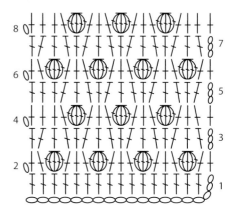

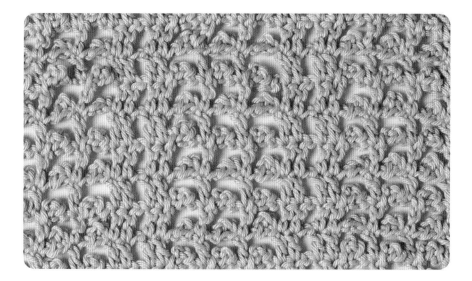

Fancy Picot Stitch

Multiple of 10 sts + 1.

(add 2 for base chain)

1st row (right side): Skip 3ch (count as 1dc), *1dc into each of next 2ch, work a picot of [3ch, insert hook down through top of last st made and sl st to close], [1ch, skip 1ch, 1dc into next ch, picot] twice, 1ch, skip 1ch, 1dc into each of next 2ch**, 1ch, skip 1ch; rep from * ending last rep at **, 1dc into last ch, turn.

2nd row: 3ch (count as 1dc), skip first st, *1dc into each of next 2 sts, [picot, 1ch, skip next ch and picot, 1dc into next dc] 3 times, 1dc into next dc**, 1ch, skip 1ch; rep from * ending last rep at **, 1dc into top of tch, turn.

Rep 2nd row.

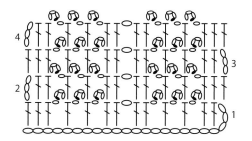

Sieve Stitch

Multiple of 2 sts + 1.

(add 1 for base chain)

Base row (wrong side): 1sc into 2nd ch from hook, *1ch, skip 1ch, 1sc into next ch; rep from * to end, turn.

Commence Pattern

1st row: 1ch, skip 1 st, *2sc into next ch sp, skip next sc; rep from * until 1 ch sp remains, 1sc into last ch sp, 1sc into next sc, skip tch, turn.

2nd row: 1ch, skip 1 st, 1sc into next st, *1ch, skip 1 st, 1sc into next sc; rep from * until only tch remains, 1sc into tch, turn.

3rd row: 1ch, skip first 2 sts, *2sc into next ch sp, skip next sc; rep from * until only tch remains, 2sc into tch, turn.

4th row: As 2nd row.

5th row: 1ch, 1sc into first st, *skip next sc, 2sc into next ch sp; rep from * ending last rep in tch, turn.

6th row: 1ch, skip 1 st, *1sc into next sc, 1ch, skip 1sc; rep from * ending 1sc into tch, turn.

7th row: 1ch, skip 1 st, 1sc into next ch sp, *skip 1sc, 2sc into next sp; rep from * ending skip last sc, 1sc into tch, turn.

8th row: 1ch, 1sc into first st, *1ch, skip 1sc, 1sc into next st; rep from * to end working last st into top of tch, turn.

Rep these 8 rows.

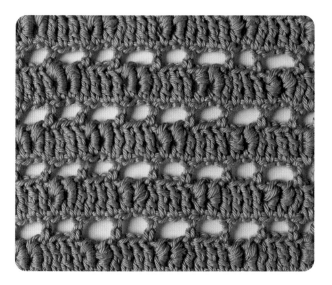

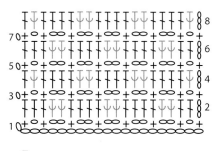

Bullion st with (yo) 7 times

Bullion Diagonals

Multiple of 6 sts + 2.

(add 1 for base chain)

Special Abbreviation: Bullion Stitch = Wrap the yarn over the hook as many times as specified; insert the hook as required; wrap the yarn once again and draw a loop through; wrap the yarn again and draw through all the loops on the hook, picking them off one at a time, if necessary; work a chain to complete the bullion stitch.

1st row (wrong side): 1sc into 2nd ch from hook, 1ch, skip 1ch, 1sc into next ch, *2ch, skip 2ch, 1sc into next ch; rep from * to last 2ch, 1ch, skip 1ch, 1sc into last ch, turn.

2nd row: 3ch (count as 1dc), skip first st, 1dc into next ch sp, *1dc into next sc, 1 Bullion st into each of next 2ch, 1dc into next sc**, 1dc into each of next 2ch; rep from *

ending last rep at ** when 1 ch sp remains, 1dc into next ch, 1dc into last sc, skip tch, turn.

3rd row: 1ch, 1sc into first st, 1ch, skip 1 st, 1sc into next st, *2ch, skip 2 sts, 1sc into next st; rep from * to last 2 sts, 1ch, skip 1 st, 1sc into top of tch, turn.

4th row: 3ch (count as 1dc), skip first st, 1 Bullion st into next ch sp, *1dc into next sc, 1dc into each of next 2ch, 1dc into next sc**, 1 Bullion st into each of next 2ch; rep from * ending last rep at ** when 1ch sp remains, 1 Bullion st into next sp, 1dc into last sc, skip tch, turn.

5th row: As 3rd row.

Rep 2nd to 5th rows.

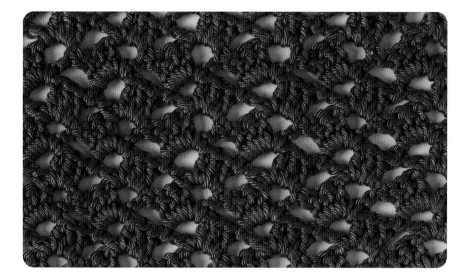

Rover Stitch

Multiple of 6 sts + 5.

1st row (right side): Work 1dc into 6th ch from hook, 1dc into each of next 2ch, 3ch, 1dc into next ch, *skip 2ch, 1dc into each of next 3ch, 3ch, 1dc into next ch; rep from * to last 2ch, skip 1ch, 1dc into last ch, turn.

2nd row: 3ch (count as 1dc), *into next 3ch arch work [3dc, 3ch, 1dc]; rep from * to last 3dc, skip 3dc, 1dc into next ch, turn.

3rd row: 3ch, *into next 3ch arch work [3dc, 3ch, 1dc]; rep from * to last 4dc, skip 3dc, 1dc into 3rd of 3ch at beg of previous row, turn.

Rep 3rd row.

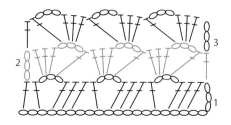

Mix neutral, natural colors and texture with intense color to add impact to home décor projects. This works well for cushions and throws when complemented by grainy wood, leather or linen in the home.

Winkle Picot Stitch

Multiple of 3 sts + 2.

(add 4 for base chain)

1st row (right side): 1sc into 6th ch from hook, *skip 1ch, 1sc into next ch, 3ch, 1sc into next ch; rep from * until 3ch remain, skip 1ch, 1sc into next ch, 2ch, 1hdc into last ch, turn.

2nd row: 4ch, 1sc into next 2ch sp, *[1sc, 3ch, 1sc] into next 3ch arch; rep from * ending [1sc, 2ch, 1hdc] into last ch arch, turn.

Rep 2nd row.

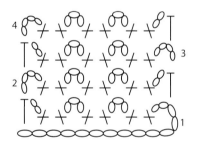

Relief Squares

Multiple of 10 sts + 4.

(add 1 for base chain)

Special Abbreviation: Dtr/rf (raised double treble crochet at the front of the fabric) = Wrap the yarn around the hook, insert the hook from in front and from right to left around the stem of the appropriate stitch, and complete the stitch normally.

Dtr/rb (raised double treble crochet at the back of the fabric) = Wrap the yarn around the hook, insert the hook from behind and from right to left around the stem of the appropriate stitch, and complete the stitch normally.

1st base row (right side): Using A, 1sc into 2nd ch from hook, 1sc into next and each ch to end, turn.

2nd base row: 1 ch, 1sc into first and each st to end, skip tch, turn.

Commence Pattern

Change to B and rep the 2nd base row twice.

Change to C and rep the 2nd base row 4 times.

7th row: Using B, 1ch, 1sc into each of first 3 sts, *[1dtr/rf around st corresponding to next st 5 rows below, i.e. last row worked in B] twice, 1sc into each of next 4 sts, [1dtr/rf around st corresponding to next st 5 rows below] twice, 1sc into each of next 2 sts; rep from * ending 1sc into last st, skip tch, turn.

8th row: Using B rep 2nd base row.

9th row: Using A, 1ch, 1sc into first st, *[1quin tr/rf around st corresponding to next st 9 rows below, i.e. last row worked in A] twice, 1sc into each of next 8 sts; rep from * to last 3 sts, [1quin tr/rf around st corresponding to next st 9 rows below] twice, 1sc into last st, skip tch, turn.

10th row: Using A rep 2nd base row.

Rep these 10 rows.

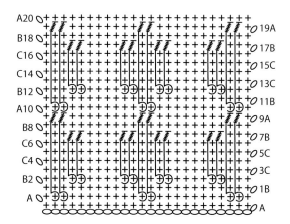

Half Double Crochet V Stitch

Multiple of 2 sts.

(add 2 for base chain)

1st row (right side): [1hdc, 1ch, 1hdc] into 4th ch from hook, *skip 1ch, [1hdc, 1ch, 1hdc] into next ch; rep from * until 2ch remain, skip 1ch, 1hdc into last ch, turn.

2nd row: 2ch, *skip 2 sts, [1hdc, 1ch, 1hdc] into next ch sp; rep from * to last hdc, skip 1 st, 1hdc into tch, turn.

Rep 2nd row.

Twin V Stitch

Multiple of 4 sts + 2.

(add 2 for base chain)

1st row (right side): 2dc into 5th ch from hook, 2dc into next ch, *skip 2ch, 2dc into each of next 2ch; rep from * to last 2ch, skip 1ch, 1dc into last ch, turn.

2nd row: 3ch, *skip 2 sts, 2dc into each of next 2 sts; rep from * to last 2 sts, skip 1 st, 1dc into tch, turn.

Rep 2nd row.

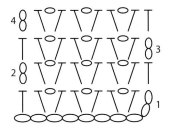

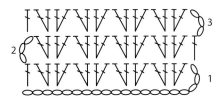

Popcorn Waffle Stitch

Multiple of 4 sts + 1.

(add 1 for base chain)

1st row (right side): 1sc into 2nd ch from hook, *3ch, 5dc popcorn into same place as previous sc, skip 3ch, 1sc into next ch; rep from * to end, turn.

2nd row: 3ch (count as 1dc), skip first st, *1sc into each of next 2ch, 1hdc into next ch, 1dc into next sc; rep from * to end, skip tch, turn.

3rd row: 1ch, 1sc into first st, *3ch, 5dc popcorn into same place as previous sc, skip next 3 sts, 1sc into next dc; rep from * ending last rep in top of tch, turn.

Rep 2nd and 3rd rows.

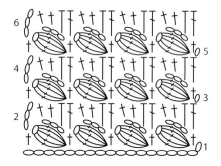

Bridge Stitch

Multiple of 5 sts + 2.

1st row (right side): Work 1sc into 2nd ch from hook, *5ch, skip 4ch, 1sc into next ch; rep from * to end, turn.

2nd row: 1ch, work 1sc into first sc, *5sc into 5ch sp, 1sc into next sc; rep from * to end, turn.

3rd row: 3ch (count as 1dc), skip first sc, work 1dc into each of next 5sc, *1ch, skip 1sc, 1dc into each of next 5sc; rep from * to last sc, 1dc into last sc, turn.

4th row: 1ch, 1sc into first dc, *5ch, 1sc into next ch sp; rep from * to end placing last sc into 3rd of 3ch at beg of previous row, turn.

Rep 2nd to 4th rows.

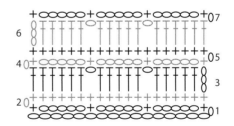

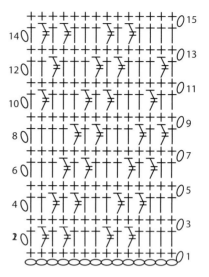

Diagonal Trip Stitch

Multiple of 6 sts + 2.

(add 1 for base chain)

1st row (right side): 1sc into 2nd ch from hook, 1sc into each ch to end, turn.

2nd row: 1ch, 1sc into first st, *1tr into next st, 1sc into next st, 1tr into next st, 1sc into each of next 3 sts; rep from * ending 1sc into last sc, skip tch, turn.

3rd row: 1ch, 1sc into first st, 1sc into next and each st to end, skip tch, turn.

4th row: 1ch, 1sc into each of first 2 sts, *1tr into next st, 1sc into next st, 1tr into next st, 1sc into each of next 3 sts; rep from * to end, skip tch, turn.

5th row: As 3rd row.

6th row: 1ch, 1sc into each of first 3 sts, *1tr into next st, 1sc into next st, 1tr into next st, 1sc into each of next 3 sts; rep from * to end, omitting 1sc at end of last rep, skip tch, turn.

Continue in this way, working the pairs of tr 1 st further to the left on every wrong-side row.

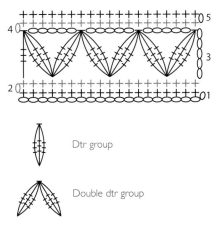

Dtr group

Double dtr group

Two-leaf Bar

Multiple of 6 sts + 2.

Special Abbreviations: Dtr group = work 3dtr into next sc until 1 loop of each remains on hook, yo and through all 4 loops on hook.

Double dtr group = work 3dtr into same sc as last group until 1 loop of each remains on hook (4 loops on hook), skip 5sc, into next sc work 3dtr until 1 loop of each remains on hook, yo and through all 7 loops on hook.

1st row (right side): Work 1sc into 2nd ch from hook, 1sc into each ch to end, turn.

2nd row: 1ch, work 1sc into each sc to end, turn.

3rd row: 5ch (count as 1dtr), skip first 3sc, work 1dtr group into next sc, 5ch, *1 double dtr group, 5ch; rep from * to last 3sc, into same sc as last group work 3dtr until 1 loop of each remains on hook (4 loops on hook), 1dtr into last sc until 5 loops remain on hook, yo and through all 5 loops, turn.

4th row: 1ch, 1sc into top of first group, 5sc into 5ch arch, *1sc into top of next group, 5sc into next 5ch arch; rep from * to last group, 1sc into top of last group, turn.

5th row: 1ch, work 1sc into each sc to end, turn.

Rep 2nd to 5th rows.

Double Crochet V

Multiple of 2 sts.

(add 2 for base chain)

1st row (right side): 2dc into 4th ch from hook, *skip 1ch, 2dc into next ch; rep from * to last 2ch, skip 1ch, 1dc into last ch, turn.

2nd row: 3ch, *skip 2 sts, 2dc between 2nd skipped st and next st; rep from * to last 2 sts, skip 1 st, 1dc into top of tch, turn.

Rep 2nd row.

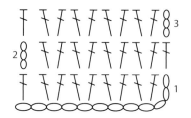

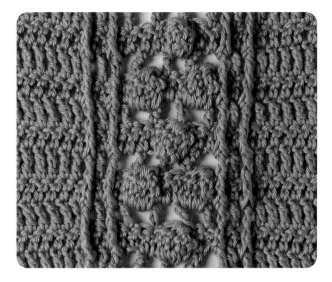

Bobble Braid Stitch

Worked over 13 sts on a background of any number of sts worked in basic double crochet on right-side rows and single crochet on wrong-side rows.

Special Abbreviation: Tr/rf (raised treble crochet at the front of the fabric) = Wrap the yarn around the hook, insert the hook from in front and from right to left around the stem of the appropriate stitch, and complete the stitch normally.

Tr/rb (raised treble crochet at the back of the fabric) = Wrap the yarn around the hook, insert the hook from behind and from right to left around the stem of the appropriate stitch, and complete the stitch normally.

1st row (right side): 1dc into each of first 4 sts, [1ch, skip 1 st, 1dc into next st] 3 times, 1dc into each of last 3 sts.

2nd row: 1sc into each of first 4 sts, work dc5tog into next ch sp, 1sc into next dc, 1sc into next sp, 1sc into next dc, dc5tog into next sp, 1sc into each of last 4 sts.

3rd row: 1tr/rf around first st 2 rows below (i.e: 1st row), 1dc into next st on previous (i.e: 2nd) row, 1tr/rf around next st 2 rows below, [1ch, skip 1 st, 1dc into next st on previous row] 3 times, 1ch, skip 1 st, 1tr/rf around next st 2 rows below, 1dc into next st on previous row, 1tr/rf around next st 2 rows below.

4th row: 1sc into each of first 6 sts, work dc5tog into next st, 1sc into each of last 6 sts.

5th row: [1tr/rf around corresponding raised st 2 rows below, 1dc into next st] twice, [1ch, skip 1 st, 1dc into next st] 3 times, 1tr/rf around corresponding raised st 2 rows below, 1dc into next st, 1tr/rf around corresponding raised st 2 rows below.

Rep 2nd to 5th rows.

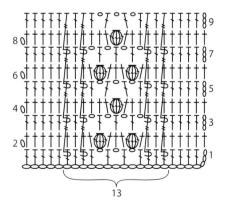

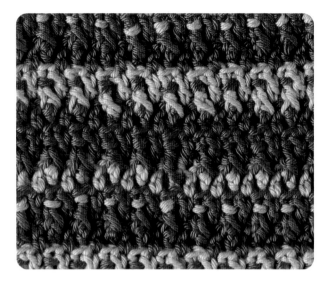

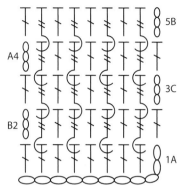

Interweave Stitch

Multiple of 2 sts + 1.

(add 2 for base chain)

Note: Work 1 row each in colors A, B, and C throughout.

Special Abbreviation: Tr/rf (raised treble crochet at the front of the fabric) = Wrap the yarn around the hook, insert the hook from in front and from right to left around the stem of the appropriate stitch, and complete the stitch normally.

Tr/rb (raised treble crochet at the back of the fabric) = Wrap the yarn around the hook, insert the hook from behind and from right to left around the stem of the appropriate stitch, and complete the stitch normally.

1st row (right side): Skip 3ch (count as 1dc), 1dc into next and each ch to end, turn.

2nd row: 3ch (count as 1dc), skip first st, *1tr/rf around next st, 1dc into next st; rep from * ending last rep in top of tch, turn.

Rep 2nd row.

Three-and-Two Stitch

Multiple of 6 sts + 2.

(add 2 for base chain)

1st row (right side): Work a V st of [1dc, 1ch, 1dc] into 5th ch from hook, *skip 2ch, 3dc into next ch, skip 2ch, work a V st into next ch; rep from * to last 5ch, skip 2ch, 3dc into next ch, skip 1ch, 1dc into last ch, turn.

2nd row: 3ch, *skip 2 sts, work 3dc into center dc of next 3dc, work a V st into ch sp at center of next V st; rep from * ending 1dc into top of tch, turn.

3rd row: 3ch, *V st into sp of next V st, 3dc into center dc of next 3dc; rep from * ending 1dc into top of tch, turn.

Rep 2nd and 3rd rows.

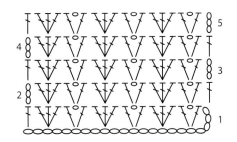

Curve Fan Stitch

Multiple of 6 sts + 3.

Special Abbreviations: Dc2tog = work 1dc into each of next 2 sts until 1 loop of each remains on hook, yo and through all 3 loops on hook.

Half Cluster = work 1dc into each of next 3 sts until 1 loop of each remains on hook, yo and through all 4 loops on hook.

Cluster = work 1dc into each of next 5 sts until 1 loop of each remains on hook, yo and through all 6 loops on hook.

1st row (right side): Work dc2tog working into 4th and 5th ch from hook, *3ch, 1sc into next ch, turn, 1ch, 1sc into last sc worked, 3sc into last 3ch sp formed, [turn, 1ch, 1sc into each of the 4sc] 3 times, work 1 cluster over

next 5ch; rep from * to end, working half cluster at end of last rep, turn.

2nd row: 4ch (count as 1tr), work 2tr into top of first half cluster; skip 3sc, 1sc into next sc, *5tr into top of next cluster; skip 3sc, 1sc into next sc; rep from * to last dc2tog, 3tr into top of 3ch at beg of previous row, turn.

3rd row: 3ch (count as 1dc), skip first tr, work dc2tog over next 2tr, *3ch, 1sc into next sc, turn, 1ch, 1sc into last sc worked, 3sc into last 3ch sp formed, [turn, 1ch, 1sc into each of the 4sc] 3 times, work 1 cluster over next 5tr; rep from * to end, and working half cluster at end of last rep placing last dc of half cluster into 4th of 4ch at beg of previous row, turn.

Rep 2nd and 3rd rows, ending with a 2nd row.

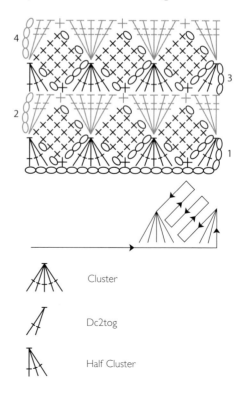

Cluster
Dc2tog
Half Cluster

Interlocking Shell Stitch

Multiple of 6 sts + 1.

(add 2 for base chain)

Note: Work 1 row each in colors A and B alternately; fasten off each color at the end of each row.

1st row (right side): Skip 2ch (count as 1dc), 2dc into next ch, skip 2ch, 1sc into next ch, *skip 2ch, 5dc into next ch, skip 2ch, 1sc into next ch; rep from * to last 3ch, skip 2ch, 3dc into last ch, turn.

2nd row: 1ch, 1sc into first st, *2ch, dc5tog over next 5 sts, 2ch, 1sc into next st; rep from * ending last rep in top of tch, turn.

3rd row: 3ch (count as 1dc), 2dc into first st, skip 2ch, 1sc into next cluster, *skip 2ch, 5dc into next sc, skip 2ch, 1sc into next cluster; rep from * to last 2ch, skip 2ch, 3dc into last sc, skip tch, turn.

Rep 2nd and 3rd rows.

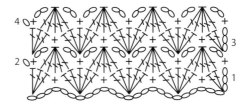

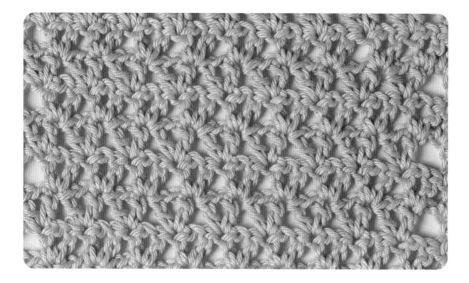

Offset V Stitch

Multiple of 3 sts + 1.

(add 3 for base chain)

1st row (right side): 1dc into 4th ch from hook, *skip 2ch, work a V st of [1dc, 1ch, 1dc] into next ch; rep from * to last 3ch, skip 2ch, 1dc into last ch, turn.

2nd row: 4ch, 1dc into first st, *V st into 2nd dc of next V st; rep from * until 1dc and tch remain, skip 1dc and 1ch, 1dc into next ch, turn.

Rep 2nd row.

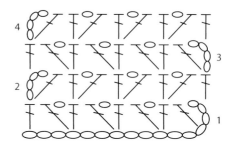

Bar Stitch

Multiple of 3 sts + 3.

Special Abbreviation: 1dc/rf = work 1dc around stem of next st 2 rows below, inserting hook around stem from right to left to draw up loops.

1st row (right side): Work 1sc into 2nd ch from hook, 1sc into each ch to end, turn.

2nd row: 1ch, work 1sc into each sc to end, turn.

3rd row: 1ch, work 1sc into each of first 2sc, *1dc/rf around next sc 2 rows below, 1sc into each of next 2sc; rep from * to end, turn.

4th row: 1ch, work 1sc into each st to end, turn.

5th row: 1ch, work 1sc into each of first 2sc, *1dc/rf around stem of next dc/rf 2 rows below, 1sc into each of next 2sc; rep from * to end, turn.

Rep 4th and 5th rows.

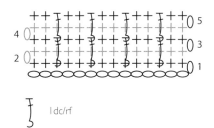

1dc/rf

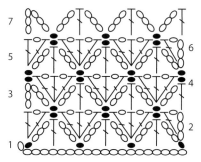

Interlocking Diamonds

Multiple of 6 sts + 1.

(add 1 for base chain)

Work 1st row in color A, then 2 rows each in colors B and A alternately throughout.

1st row (wrong side): Sl st into 2nd ch from hook, *3ch, skip 2ch, 1dc into next ch, 3ch, skip 2ch, sl st into next ch; rep from * to end, turn.

2nd row: 4ch (count as 1dc and 1ch), 1dc into first sl st, *skip 3ch, sl st into next dc**, skip 3ch, work [1dc, 1ch, 1dc, 1ch, 1dc] into next sl st; rep from * ending last rep at ** in last dc, skip 3ch, work [1dc, 1ch, 1dc] into last sl st, turn.

3rd row: 6ch (count as 1dc and 3ch), skip [first st, 1ch and 1dc], *sl st into next sl st**, 3ch, skip 1dc and 1ch, 1dc into next dc, 3ch, skip 1ch and 1dc; rep from * ending last rep at ** in last sl st, 3ch, skip 1dc and 1ch, 1dc into next ch to tch, turn.

4th row: Sl st into first st, *skip 3ch, [1dc, 1ch, 1dc, 1ch, 1dc] all into next sl st, skip 3ch, sl st into next dc; rep from * ending in 3rd ch of tch loop, turn.

5th row: *3ch, skip 1dc and 1ch, 1dc into next dc, 3ch, skip 1ch and 1dc, sl st into next sl st; rep from * to end, turn.

Rep 2nd to 5th rows.

Picot V Stitch

Multiple of 3 sts + 1.

(add 2 for base chain)

1st row (right side): Skip 3ch (count as 1dc), 1dc into next ch, skip 1ch, 1dc into next ch, work a picot of [3ch, insert hook down through top of dc just made and work a sl st], 1dc into same ch as last dc, *skip 2ch, [1dc, picot, 1dc] into next ch; rep from * to last 3ch, skip 2ch, 1dc into last ch, turn.

2nd row: 3ch (count as 1dc), 1dc into first st, *skip 1dc and picot, [1dc, picot, 1dc] into next dc; rep from * to last 2 sts, skip next dc, 1dc into top of tch, turn.

Rep 2nd row.

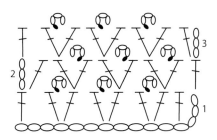

3rd row: I ch, work Isc into each of first 2sc, Idc/rf, Isc into next sc, Idc/rf, *Isc into each of next 4sc, I puff st into next sc, Isc into each of next 4sc, Idc/rf, Isc into next sc, Idc/rf; rep from * to last 2sc, Isc into each of last 2sc, turn.

5th row: I ch, work Isc into each of first 2sc, Idc/rf, Isc into next sc, Idc/rf, *Isc into each of next 2sc, I puff st into next sc, Isc into each of next 3sc, I puff st into next sc, Isc into each of next 2sc, Idc/rf, Isc into next sc, Idc/rf; rep from * to last 2sc, Isc into each of last 2sc, turn.

7th row: As 3rd row.

9th row: I ch, Isc into each of first 2sc, Idc/rf, Isc into next sc, Idc/rf, *Isc into each of next 9sc, Idc/rf, Isc into next sc, Idc/rf; rep from * to last 2sc, Isc into each of last 2sc, turn.

Rep 2nd to 9th rows.

Dot and Bar Stitch

Multiple of 12 sts + 8.

Special Abbreviations: Puff st = *yo, insert hook into next st, yo and draw a loop through; rep from * 4 times more, inserting hook into same st as before (11 loops on hook), yo and draw through 10 loops, yo and draw through 2 remaining loops.

Idc/rf = work Idc around stem of next st 2 rows below, inserting hook around stem from right to left to draw up loops.

1st row (right side): Work Isc into 2nd ch from hook, Isc into each ch to end, turn.

2nd and every alt row: I ch, work Isc into each st to end, turn.

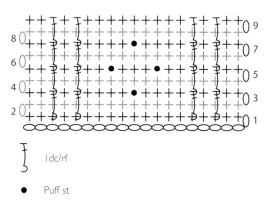

$\overline{\mathfrak{Z}}$ I dc/rf

●   Puff st

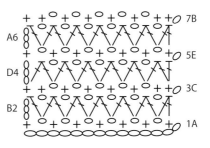

Zig-Zag Pip Stitch

Multiple of 4 sts + 1.

(add 1 for base chain)

Note: Work 1 row each in colors A, B, C, D, and E throughout.

1st row (right side): 1sc into 2nd ch from hook, *1ch, skip 1ch, 1sc into next ch; rep from * to end, turn.

2nd row: 3ch, 1dc into next ch sp (counts as dc2tog), *1ch, dc2tog inserting hook into same sp as previous st for first leg and into next sp for 2nd leg; rep from * to last sp, ending 1ch, dc2tog over same sp and last sc, skip tch, turn.

3rd row: 1ch, 1sc into first st, *1sc into next sp, 1ch, skip next cluster; rep from * ending 1sc into last sp, 1sc into last st, skip tch, turn.

4th row: 3ch (count as 1dc), dc2tog inserting hook into first st for first leg and into next sp for 2nd leg, *1ch, dc2tog inserting hook into same sp as previous st for first leg and into next sp for 2nd leg; rep from * ending with 2nd leg of last cluster in last sc, 1dc into same place, skip tch, turn.

5th row: 1ch, 1sc into first st, *1ch, skip next cluster, 1sc into next sp; rep from * working last sc into top of tch, turn.

Rep 2nd to 5th rows.

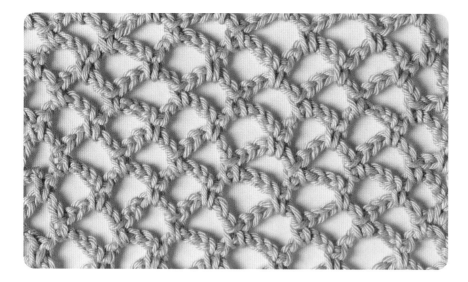

Plain Trellis Stitch

Multiple of 4 sts + 3.

(add 3 for base chain)

1st row: 1sc into 6th ch from hook, *5ch, skip 3ch, 1sc into next ch; rep from * to end, turn.

2nd row: *5ch, 1sc into next 5ch arch; rep from * to end, turn.

Rep 2nd row.

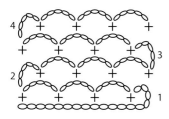

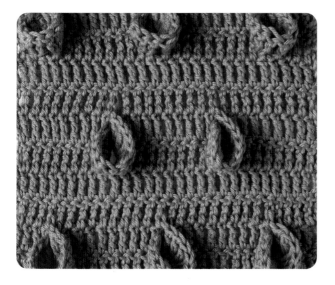

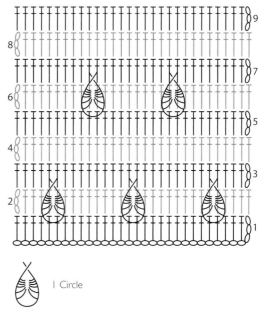

1 Circle

Half Moon Stitch

Multiple of 10 sts +12.

Special Abbreviation: 1 Circle = rotating work as required, work 6dc down and around stem of next dc 1 row below, then work 6dc up and around stem of previous dc 1 row below.

1st row (right side): Work 1dc into 4th ch from hook, 1dc into each ch to end, turn.

2nd row: 3ch (count as 1dc), skip first dc, work 1dc into each dc to end, working last dc into 3rd of 3ch at beg of previous row, turn.

3rd row: 3ch, skip first dc, work 1dc into each of next 4dc, *work 1 circle, working behind circle work 1dc into each of next 10dc; rep from * to end, omitting 5dc at end of last rep and working last dc into 3rd of 3ch at beg of previous row, turn.

4th, 5th, and 6th rows: 3ch, skip first dc, work 1dc into each dc to end, working last dc into 3rd of 3ch at beg of previous row, turn.

7th row: 3ch, skip first dc, work 1dc into each of next 9dc, *work 1 circle, 1dc into each of next 10dc; rep from * to end, working last dc into 3rd of 3ch, turn.

8th and 9th rows: 3ch, skip first dc, work 1dc into each dc to end working last dc into 3rd of 3ch, turn.

Rep 2nd to 9th rows.

Aligned Railing Stitch

Multiple of 2 sts + 1.

(add 2 for base chain)

On a background of basic double crochets in color M, work raised rows—one row each in colors A, B, and C throughout.

Note: Work 2 rows basic double crochet in M.

Special Abbreviation: Tr/rf (raised treble crochet at the front of the fabric) = Wrap the yarn around the hook, insert the hook from in front and from right to left around the stem of the appropriate stitch, and complete the stitch normally.

Tr/rb (raised treble crochet at the back of the fabric) = Wrap the yarn around the hook, insert the hook from behind and from right to left around the stem of the appropriate stitch, and complete the stitch normally.

Commence Pattern

1st row (right side): Put working loop temporarily on a stitch holder or safety pin, draw loop of contrast color through top of last background st completed, 1ch, work 1tr/rf around stem of 2nd st in second-to-last row, *1ch, skip 1 st, 1tr/rf around stem of next st in second-to-last row; rep from * ending sl st into top of tch at beg of last background row worked. Fasten off, but do not turn work.

2nd row: Replace hook in working loop of M. 3ch, work 1dc inserting hook through top of raised st and background st at the same time, *work 1dc inserting hook under contrast color ch and top of next st in background color at the same time, work 1dc inserting hook under top of next raised st and background st as before; rep from * to tch, 1dc in top of tch.

Work 1 row in basic double crochet.

Rep these 3 rows.

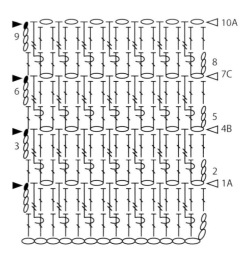

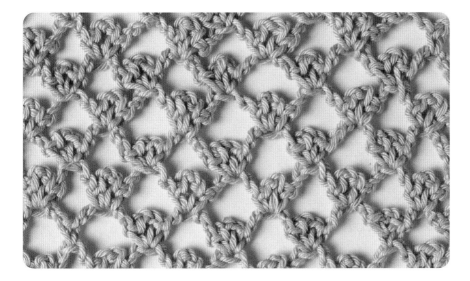

Picot Trellis Stitch

Multiple of 5 sts + 1.

(add 1 for base chain)

1st row: 1sc into 2nd ch from hook, *5ch, skip 4ch, 1sc into next ch; rep from * to end, turn.

2nd row: *5ch, work a picot of [1sc, 3ch, 1sc] into 3rd ch of next 5ch arch; rep from * ending 2ch, 1dc into last sc, skip tch, turn.

3rd row: 1ch, 1sc into first st, *5ch, skip picot, picot into 3rd ch of next 5ch arch; rep from * ending 5ch, skip picot, 1sc into tch arch, turn.

Rep 2nd and 3rd rows.

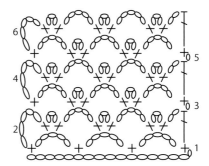

Oval Cluster Stitch

Multiple of 10 sts + 10.

Special Abbreviations: Lower Cluster = work 5tr into next skipped sc 2 rows below.

Upper Cluster = *[yo] twice then insert hook from right to left around stem of next tr 2 rows below, work 1tr in usual way until last loop of tr remains on hook; rep from * 4 times more, yo and through all 6 loops.

Note: Count each ch sp as 1 st throughout.

1st row (right side): Work 1sc into 2nd ch from hook, 1sc into each ch to end, turn.

2nd row: 3ch (count as 1dc), skip first sc, work 1dc into each of next 3sc, *1ch, skip 1sc, 1dc into each of next 9 sts; rep from * to end omitting 5dc at end of last rep, turn.

3rd row: 1ch, work 1sc into each of first 2dc, *work lower cluster, skip 5 sts of previous row, 1sc into each of next 5dc; rep from * to end, omitting 3sc at end of last rep and placing last sc into 3rd of 3ch at beg of previous row, turn.

4th row: 3ch, skip first sc, work 1dc into each st to end, turn.

5th row: 1ch, work 1sc into each of first 4dc, *work upper cluster over next 5tr 2 rows below, skip next dc on previous row, 1sc into each of next 9dc; rep from * to end, omitting 5sc at end of last rep and placing last sc into 3rd of 3ch at beg of previous row, turn.

6th row: 3ch, skip first sc, work 1dc into each of next 8 sts, *1ch, skip 1sc, 1dc into each of next 9 sts; rep from * to end.

7th row: 1ch, work 1sc into each of first 7dc, *work lower cluster, skip 5 sts of previous row, 1sc into each of next 5dc; rep from * to last 2dc, 1sc into each of last 2dc, working last sc into 3rd of 3ch at beg of previous row, turn.

8th row: 3ch, skip first sc, work 1dc into each st to end, turn.

9th row: 1ch, work 1sc into each of first 9dc, *work upper cluster over next 5tr 2 rows below, skip next dc on previous row, 1sc into each of next 9dc; rep from * to end placing last sc into 3rd of 3ch at beg of previous row, turn.

Rep 2nd to 9th rows.

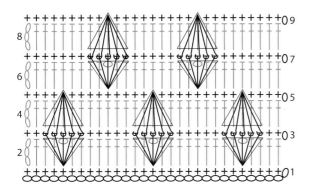

Upper cluster

Lower cluster

2nd row (right side in B): Join yarn into first st, 1ch, 1sc into first st, *3ch, skip 3ch, 1sc into next puff st, 3ch, skip 3ch, 1sc into next sc; rep from * to end, turn.

3rd row (wrong side in A): 6ch (count as 1dc and 3ch), skip first st and 3ch, 1sc into next sc, *3ch, skip 3ch, puff st into next sc, 3ch, skip 3ch, 1sc into next sc; rep from * ending 3ch, skip 3ch, 1dc into last sc. Do not turn.

4th row (wrong side in B): Pick up yarn in 3rd ch of tch, 1ch, 1sc into same place, *3ch, skip 3ch, 1sc into next sc, 3ch, skip 3ch, 1sc into next st; rep from * to end, turn.

5th row (right side in A): 1ch, 1sc into first st, *3ch, skip 3ch, puff st into next sc, 3ch, skip 3ch, 1sc into next sc; rep from * to end. Do not turn.

Rep 2nd to 5th rows.

Shadow Tracery Stitch

Multiple of 6 sts + 1.

(add 1 for base chain)

Special Abbreviation: Puff stitch = work hdc5tog all into same place ending with 1ch drawn tightly to close.

Note: Work 1 row each in colors A and B alternately throughout. Do not break yarn when changing color, but fasten off temporarily and begin row at same end as new color.

1st row (right side in A): 1sc into 2nd ch from hook, *3ch, skip 2ch, puff st into next ch, 3ch, skip 2ch, 1sc into next ch; rep from * to end. Do not turn.

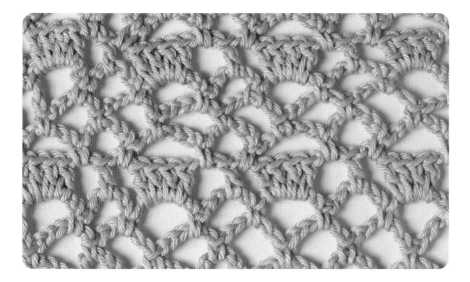

Block Trellis Stitch

Multiple of 8 sts + 5.

(add 1 for base chain)

1st row (right side): 1sc into 2nd ch from hook, *5ch, skip 3ch, 1sc into next ch; rep from * to end, turn.

2nd row: *5ch, 1sc into next 5ch arch; rep from * ending 2ch, 1dc into last sc, skip tch, turn.

3rd row: 3ch (count as 1dc), 1dc into first st, 2ch, 1dc into next 5ch arch, *2ch, 4dc into next arch, 2ch, 1dc into next arch; rep from * to end, turn.

4th row: *5ch, 1sc into next 2ch sp; rep from * ending 2ch, 1dc into top of tch, turn.

5th row: 1ch, 1sc into first st, *5ch, 1sc into next 5ch arch; rep from * to end, turn.

Rep 2nd to 5th rows.

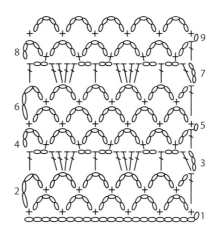

Quiver Stitch

Multiple of 4 sts + 4

Special Abbreviation: Tr2tog 3 rows below = work 1tr into same st as last tr until last loop of tr remains on hook, skip 3 sts, work 1tr into next skipped st 3 rows below until last loop of tr remains on hook, yo and through all 3 loops. **Note:** Sts either side of tr2tog must be worked behind tr2tog.

Make required number of chains.

1st row (right side): Work 1sc into 2nd ch from hook, 1sc into each of next 2ch, *1ch, skip 1ch, 1sc into each of next 3ch; rep from * to end, turn.

2nd row: 3ch (count as 1dc), skip first sc, work 1dc into each st to end (working into actual st of each ch, not into ch sp), turn.

3rd row: 1ch, 1sc into first dc, 1tr into first skipped starting ch, skip 1dc on 2nd row, 1sc into next dc, 1ch, skip 1dc, 1sc into next dc, *tr2tog 3 rows below (into skipped starting ch), skip 1dc on 2nd row, 1sc into next dc, 1ch, skip 1dc, 1sc into next dc; rep from * to last 2dc, 1tr into same ch as 2nd leg of last tr2tog, skip 1dc, 1sc into 3rd of 3ch at beg of previous row, turn.

4th row: 3ch, skip first sc, work 1dc into each st to end, turn.

5th row: 1ch, 1sc into first dc, 1tr into next skipped dc 3 rows below, skip 1dc on previous row, 1sc into next dc, 1ch, skip 1dc, 1sc into next dc, *tr2tog 3 rows below, skip 1dc on previous row, 1sc into next dc, 1ch, skip 1dc, 1sc into next dc; rep from * to last 2dc, 1tr into same dc as 2nd leg of last tr2tog, skip 1dc, 1sc into 3rd of 3ch at beg of previous row, turn.

Rep 4th and 5th rows.

Work dc into actual st of ch on wrong-side rows, not into ch sp.

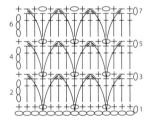

Tr2tog 3 rows below

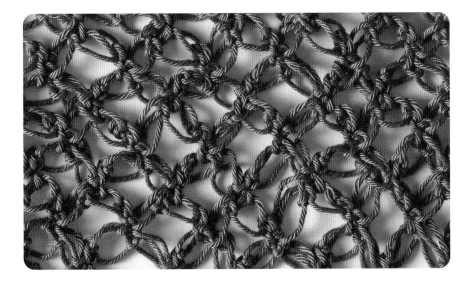

Solomon's Knot

Multiple of 2 Solomon's Knots + 1.

(add 2 Solomon's Knots for base "chain")

Special Abbreviations: ESK (Edge Solomon's Knot) =
these form the base "chain" and edges of the fabric and
are only two-thirds the length of MSK's.

MSK (Main Solomon's Knot) = these form the main
fabric and are half as long again as ESK's.

Base chain: 2ch, 1sc into 2nd ch from hook, now make
a multiple of 2ESK's (approx. ¾ in./2 cm), ending with
1MSK (approx. 1¼ in./3 cm).

1st row: 1sc into sc between 3rd and 4th loops from
hook, *2MSK, skip 2 loops, 1sc into next sc; rep from * to
end, turn.

2nd row: 2ESK and 1MSK, 1sc into sc between 4th and
5th loops from hook, *2MSK, skip 2 loops, 1sc into next
sc; rep from * ending in top of ESK, turn.

Rep 2nd row.

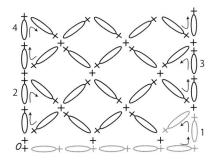

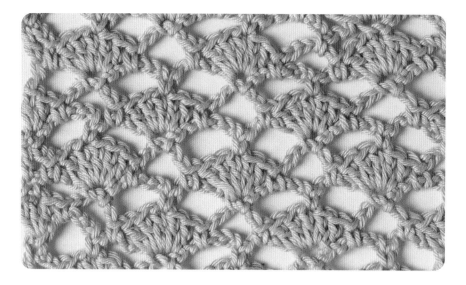

Shell Trellis Stitch

Multiple of 12 sts + 1.

(add 2 for base chain)

1st row (right side): 2dc into 3rd ch from hook, *skip 2ch, 1sc into next ch, 5ch, skip 5ch, 1sc into next ch, skip 2ch, 5dc into next ch; rep from * ending last rep with only 3dc into last ch, turn.

2nd row: 1ch, 1sc into first st, *5ch, 1sc into next 5ch arch, 5ch, 1sc into 3rd dc of next 5dc; rep from * ending last rep with 1sc into top of tch, turn.

3rd row: *5ch, 1sc into next 5ch arch, 5dc into next sc, 1sc into next arch; rep from * ending 2ch, 1dc into last sc, skip tch, turn.

4th row: 1ch, 1sc into first st, *5ch, 1sc into 3rd dc of next 5dc, 5ch, 1sc into next 5ch arch; rep from * to end, turn.

5th row: 3ch (count as 1dc), 2dc into first st, *1sc into next arch, 5ch, 1sc into next arch, 5dc into next sc; rep from * ending last rep with only 3dc into last sc, skip tch, turn.

Rep 2nd to 5th rows.

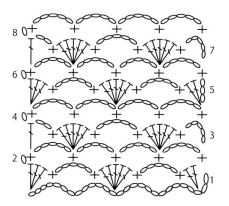

Key Tab Stitch

Multiple of 4 sts + 6.

Special Abbreviation: Cluster = work 3dc into next st until 1 loop of each remains on hook, yo and through all 4 loops on hook.

1st row (right side): Work 1 cluster into 5th ch from hook (1dc, 1ch formed at beg of row), 1ch, skip 2ch, 1sc into next ch, *3ch, 1 cluster into next ch, 1ch, skip 2ch, 1sc into next ch; rep from * to last 2ch, 2ch, 1dc into last ch, turn.

2nd row: 4ch (count as 1dc, 1ch), 1 cluster into first 2ch sp, 1ch, *1sc into next 3ch sp, 3ch, 1 cluster into same sp as last sc, 1ch; rep from * to last ch sp, 1sc into last ch sp, 2ch, 1dc into 3rd of 4ch at beg of previous row, turn. Rep 2nd row.

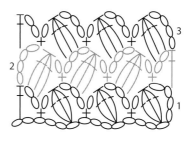

 or   Cluster

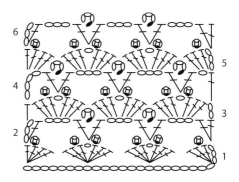

Picot Coronet Stitch

Multiple of 7 sts + 1.

(add 3 for base chain)

Work 1 row each in colors A and B alternately throughout; fasten off each color at end of each row.

1st row (right side): Skip 3ch (count as 1dc), 1dc into next ch, work a picot of [3ch, insert hook down through top of dc just made and work a sl st to close], 2dc into same ch, *skip 6ch, work a Coronet of [3dc, picot, 1ch, 1dc, picot, 2dc] into next ch; rep from * to last 7ch, skip 6ch, [3dc, picot, 1dc] into last ch, turn.

2nd row: 3ch (count as 1dc), 1dc into first st, *3ch, work a picot V st of [1dc, picot, dc] into 1ch sp at center of next Coronet; rep from * ending 3ch, 2dc into top of tch, turn.

3rd row: 2ch (count as 1hdc), skip first 2 sts, *Coronet into next 3ch sp, skip next picot V st; rep from * ending Coronet into last sp, 1hdc into top of tch, turn.

4th row: 4ch (count as 1dc and 1ch), *picot V st into sp at center of next Coronet, 3ch; rep from * ending picot V st into last Coronet, 1ch, 1dc into top of tch, turn.

5th row: 3ch (count as 1dc), skip first st, [1dc, picot, 2dc] into next ch sp, *skip next picot V st, Coronet into next sp; rep from * ending skip last picot V st, 3dc into next ch, picot, 1dc into next ch of tch, turn.

Rep 2nd to 5th rows.

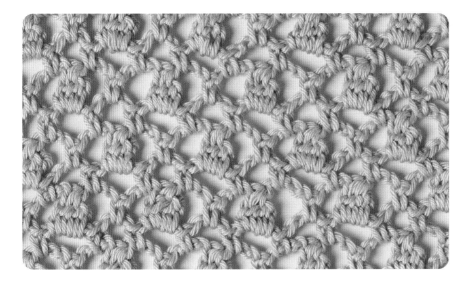

Puff Cluster Trellis Stitch

Multiple of 6 sts + 2.

(add 3 for base chain)

1st row (right side): 1sc into 5th ch from hook, *3ch, skip 2ch, 1sc into next ch; rep from * to end, turn.

2nd row: 3ch, 1sc into next 3ch arch, *3ch, hdc3tog into next arch, 3ch, 1sc into next arch; rep from * to end, turn.

3rd row: *3ch, 1sc into next 3ch arch; rep from * to end, turn.

4th row: *3ch, hdc3tog into next 3ch arch, 3ch, 1sc into next arch; rep from * ending 3ch, hdc3tog into tch arch, turn.

5th row: As 3rd row.

Rep 2nd to 5th rows.

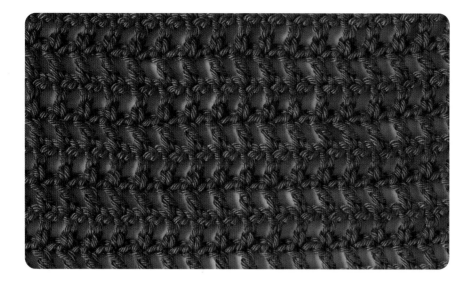

Mesh Ground 1

Multiple of 2 sts + 6.

1st row: Skip 5ch, *1dc in next ch, 1ch, skip 1ch; rep from * to last st, 1dc in last ch, turn.

2nd row: 4ch, skip first dc, *1dc in next dc, 1ch; rep from * to last st, 1dc in 3rd ch of tch, turn.

Rep 2nd row.

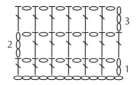

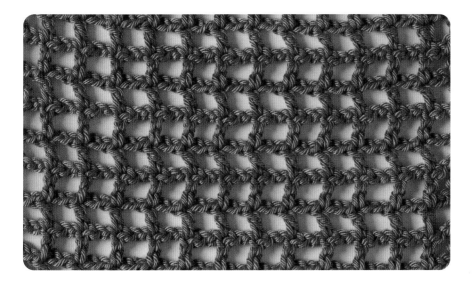

Mesh Ground II

Multiple of 3 sts + 8.

1st row: Skip 7ch, *1dc in next ch, 2ch, skip 2ch; rep from * to last st, 1dc in last ch, turn.

2nd row: 5ch, skip first dc, * 1dc in next dc, 2ch, skip 2ch; rep from * to last st, 1dc in 3rd ch of tch, turn.

Rep 2nd row.

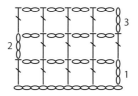

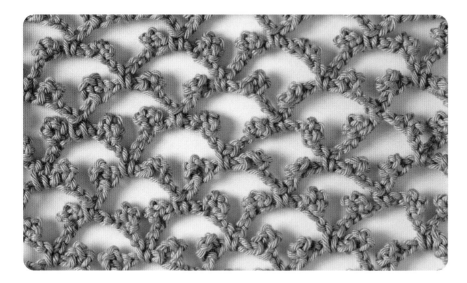

Diamond Picot Mesh

Multiple of 7 sts + 2.

1st row: Skip 1ch, 1sc in next ch, *2ch, 5ch, sl st in first of these 5ch—picot made, 3ch, 1 picot, 2ch, skip 6ch, 1sc in next ch; rep from * to end, turn.

2nd row: 2ch, 1 picot, 3ch, 1 picot, 2ch, 1sc in ch sp between picots of previous row, *2ch, 1 picot, 3ch, 1 picot, 2ch, 1sc in ch sp; rep from * to end, turn.

Rep 2nd row.

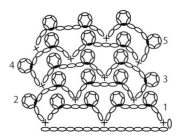

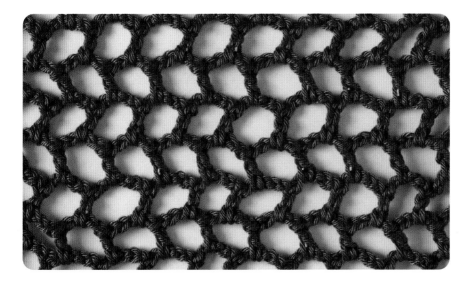

Honeycomb Mesh

Multiple of 4 sts + 10.

1st row: Skip 9ch, *1dc in next ch, 4ch, skip 3ch; rep from * to last st, 1dc, turn.

2nd row: 7ch, *1dc in 4ch sp, 4ch; rep from * to last ch sp, 1dc, turn.

Rep 2nd row.

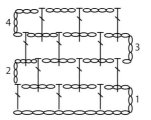

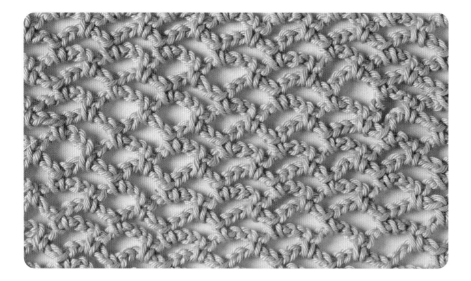

Diamond Mesh

Multiple of 4 sts + 3.

1st row: Skip 1ch, 1sc into next ch, *5ch, skip 3ch, 1sc in next ch; rep from * to last ch, in last ch, turn.

2nd row: *5ch, 1sc in next ch sp; rep from * to end, working last sc into sc, turn.

3rd row: *5ch, 1sc in next ch sp; rep from * to end, turn.

Rep 3rd row.

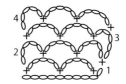

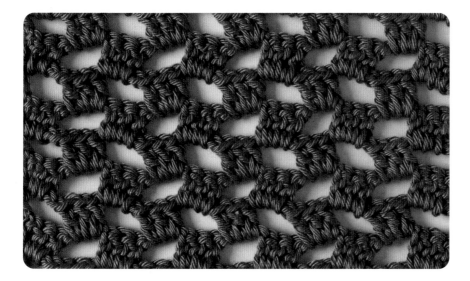

Open Checkers

Multiple of 6 sts + 9.

1st row: Skip 3ch, 1dc into each of next 2ch, *3ch, skip 3ch**, 1dc in each of next 3ch; rep from * to last ch ending at **, 1dc in last st , turn.

2nd row: 3ch, 2dc in first ch sp, *3ch, 3dc in next 3ch sp; rep from * to end, 3ch, 1dc in top of tch.

Rep 2nd row.

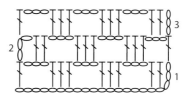

Trestle Stitch

Multiple of 4 sts + 6.

1st row: Skip 5ch, *1dc in next ch, 3ch, skip 3ch; rep from * to last ch, 1dc in last ch, turn.

2nd row: 4ch, *1sc in 2nd ch of 3ch group, 2ch, 1dc in next dc, 2ch; rep from * to last st, 1sc in tch, turn.

3rd row: 4ch, *1dc in next dc, 3ch; rep from * to last st, 1dc in tch, turn.

Rep 2nd and 3rd rows.

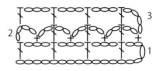

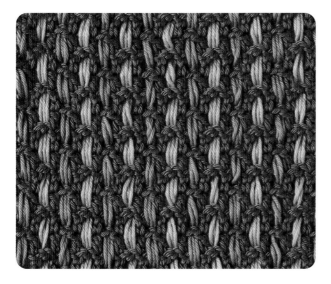

Woven Overlay

Multiple of 2 sts + 6.

1st row: Skip 5ch, *1dc in next ch, 1ch, skip 1ch; rep from * to last st, 1dc, turn.

2nd row: 4ch, skip 1 st, *1dc in next dc, 1ch; rep from * to last st, 1dc in 3rd ch, turn.

Rep 2nd row.

To weave the overlay, use 3 strands of yarn threaded in a tapestry needle. Lace the yarns vertically under and over the chain bars, filling alternate spaces on each row. Yarn should be pulled firmly so that no loops remain, yet not too tightly, or the mesh may pucker.

Chained Overlay

Multiple of 2 sts + 6.

1st row: Skip 5ch, *1dc in next ch, 1ch, skip 1ch; rep from * to last st, 1dc, turn.

2nd row: 4ch, skip 1 st, *1dc in next dc, 1ch; rep from * to last st, 1dc in 3rd ch, turn.

Rep 2nd row.

To work the overlay chains, use 2 strands of yarn; make a slip knot. With RS of mesh facing you, and yarn held behind the work, draw a loop through the first space in the lower right corner; insert hook in space directly above it, draw a loop through the space and the loop on the hook. Continue working this way to the top of the mesh, then begin again at bottom.

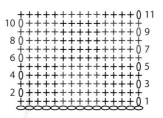

Basic Patchwork

Multiple of 5 sts + 1.

Note: The color not in use is held along the line of work and this is kept in place by the crochet stitch being worked over the yarn. This avoids ugly loops appearing on the work and also ensures that the work is completely reversible.

1st row: Using color A, into 3rd ch from hook work 1sc, 1sc into each of next 2ch, insert hook into next ch, yo and draw through a loop, yo with color B and draw through both loops on hook, using color B, work 1sc into each of next 5ch, using color A work 1sc into each of next 5ch, cont in this way working 5 sts alternately in A and B to end of row. Turn.

2nd row: Using same color as last 5sc of previous row and working over color not in use as before, work 1ch to count as first sc, 1sc into each of next 4sc, change color, 1sc into each of next 5sc, cont in this way to end of row, working last sc into turning ch. Turn.

3rd to 5th rows: Work as 2nd row.

6th to 10th rows: Work as 2nd row, working a square of color A over color B and a square of color B over color A

11th row: Work as 2nd row.

Repeat 2nd through 11th rows, ending with 5th or 10th row.

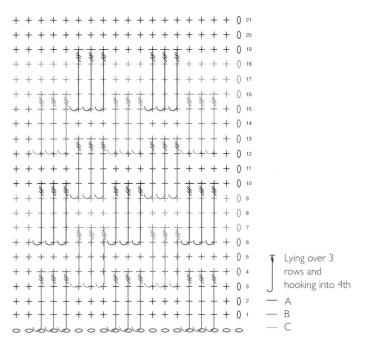

J Lying over 3 rows and hooking into 4th

— A
— B
— C

Multicolored Patchwork

Multiple of 6 sts + 7.

(add 1 for base ch).

1st row: With A, into 3rd ch from hook work 1sc, work1sc into each ch to end. Fasten off yarn. Do not turn.

2nd row: Join A to beg of previous row. 1ch to count as first sc, skip first st, 1sc into each st to end. Fasten off yarn. Do not turn.

3rd row: Work as 2nd row.

4th row: Join B to beg of previous row. 1ch to count as first sc, skip first st, 1sc into next st, yo 3 times, insert hook under horizontal front loop of next st in 4th row below, yo and draw through a loop, (yo and draw through first 2 loops on hook) 4 times – 1 surface dc has been worked , 1 surface dc into each of next 2 sts, *1sc into each of next

3 sts, 1 surface dc dc into each of next 3 sts; rep from * to last 2 sts, 1sc into each of next 2 sts. Fasten off yarn. Do not turn.

5th and 6th rows: With B work as 2nd row.

7th row: Join C to beg of previous row. 1ch to count as first sc, skip first st, 1sc into each of next 4 sts, *1 surface dc into each of next 3 sts, 1sc into each of next 3 sts; rep from * to last 2 sts, 1sc into each of last 2 sts. Fasten off yarn. Do not turn.

8th and 9th rows: With C, work as 2nd row.

10th to 12th rows: With A, work as rows 4 to 6.

13th to 15th rows: With B, work as rows 7 to 9.

16th to 18th rows: With C, work as rows 4 to 6.

19th to 21st rows: With A, work as rows 7 to 9.

Rows 4 to 21 form the pattern and color sequence.

```
+ + + + ⌇ + + + + ⌇ + + ⌇ 0  9
+ + + + ⌇ + + + + ⌇ + + ⌇ 0  8
+ + + + ⌇ + + + + ⌇ + + ⌇ 0  7
+ + + + ⌇ + + + + ⌇ + + ⌇ 0  6
+ + + + ⌇ + + + + ⌇ + + ⌇ 0  5
+ + + ⌇ + + + + ⌇ + + + ⌇ 0  4
+ + + ⌇ + + + + ⌇ + + + ⌇ 0  3
+ + + ⌇ + + + + ⌇ + + + ⌇ 0  2
+ + + + + + + + + + + + 0  1
```

⌇ Lying over 3 rows

— A

— B

Outline Squares

Multiple of 4 sts (add 1 for base ch).

Note: Unless otherwise stated, work into the back loop only of each st to end of design.

1st row: With A, into 3rd ch from hook work 1sc, 1sc into each ch to end.

Fasten off yarn. Do not turn.

2nd row: Join B to beg of previous row, 1ch to count as first sc, skip first st, 1sc into each st to end. Fasten off yarn. Do not turn work.

3rd and 4th rows: Work as 2nd row.

5th row: Join A to beg of previous row. 1ch to count as first sc, skip first st, insert hook under horizontal front loop of next st, yo and draw through a loop, (insert hook under horizontal front loop of st immediately below st just worked into, yo and draw through a loop) 3 times, (yo and draw through first 2 loops on hook) 4 times – 1 connected quad dc has been worked, *1sc into each of next 3 sts, 1 connected quad dc into next st; rep from * to last 2 sts, sc into each of next 2 sts. Fasten off yarn. Do not turn work.

6th to 8th rows: Work as 2nd row.

9th row: Join A to beg of previous row, 1ch to count as first sc, skip first st, 1sc into each of next 2 sts, *1 connected quad dc into next st, 1sc into each of next 3 sts; rep from * to last st, 1sc into last st. Fasten off yarn. Do not turn.

Rep 2nd to 9th rows.

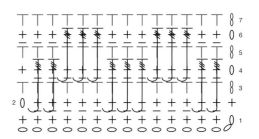

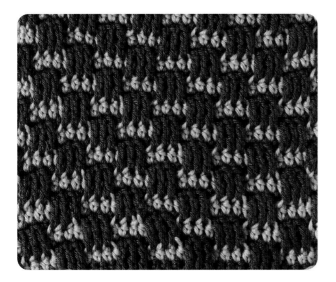

Brickwork Pattern

Multiple of 6 sts + 3.

(add 1 for base ch).

1st row: Into 3rd ch from hook work 1sc, 1sc into each ch to end, turn.

2nd row: 1ch to count as first sc, skip first sc, 1sc into front loop only of each st to end, turn. Fasten off yarn.

3rd row: Join B. 2ch to count as first hdc, skip first st, 1hdc into each st to end, placing hook under both loops. Fasten off yarn. Do not turn.

4th row: Join A to beg of previous row. 1ch to count as first sc, (1dtr into front loop only of next st in 3rd row below) twice, 1sc into back loop only of next 3 sts, *1dtr into each of next 3 sts placing the hook as before, 1sc into back loop only of next 3 sts; rep from * to last 3 sts, 1dtr into each of next 2 sts, 1sc into last st. Fasten off yarn. Do not turn work.

5th row: Work as 3rd row.

6th row: Join A to beg of previous row. 1ch to count as first sc, 1sc into back loop only of next 2 sts, *(1dtr into front loop only of next st in 3rd row below) 3 times, 1sc into back loop only of next 3 sts; rep from * to end. Fasten off. Do not turn.

7th row: Work as 3rd row.

Rep 4th through 7th rows.

Even Moss Stitch

Multiple of 2 sts.

1st row: Skip first ch, sl st into next ch, *hdc into next ch, sl st into next ch; rep from * to end, turn.

2nd row: 1 ch, skip first st, *sl st into next st, hdc into next st, rep from * ending with sl st into tch, turn.

Rep 2nd row.

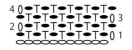

Aran Style 1

Multiple of 8 sts + 4.

1st row: Into 3rd ch from hook work 1sc, 1sc into each ch to end, turn.

2nd row: 1 ch to count as first sc, skip first st, 1sc into each st to end, turn.

3rd row: 1 ch, skip first st, 1sc into each of next 3 sts, *sl st into next st, yo and insert into next st, yo and draw through a loop, yo and draw through first loop on hook, yo and insert into same st, yo and draw through a loop, yo and draw through all loops on hook, 1 ch to secure st —berry st made, sl st into next st, 1sc into each of next 5 sts; rep from * ending last rep with 1sc into each of next 4 sts, turn.

4th row: 1 ch, skip first st, 1sc into each of next 3 sts, *1sc into next sl st, sl st into next berry st, 1sc into next sl st, 1sc into each of next 5 sts; rep from * ending last rep with 1sc into each of next 4 sts, turn.

5th row: 1ch, skip first st, 1sc into each of next 2 sts, *sl st into next sc, berry st into next sc, sl st into next sl st, berry st into next sc, sl st into next sc, 1sc into each of next 3 sts; rep from * to end, turn.

6th row: 1ch, skip first st, 1sc into each of next 3 sts, *sl st into next berry st, 1sc into next sl st, sl st into next berry st, 1sc into each of next 5 sts; rep from * ending last rep with 1sc into each of next 4 sts, turn.

7th and 8th rows: As 3rd and 4th rows.

9th row: 1ch, skip first st, berry st into next sc, sl st into next st, *1sc into each of next 5 sts, sl st into next st, berry st into next sc, sl st into next st; rep from * to end, turn.

10th row: 1ch, skip first st, sl st into next berry st, *1sc into each of next 7 sts, sl st into next berry st; rep from * ending with 1sc into last st, turn.

11th row: 1ch, skip first st, *sl st into next sl st, berry st into next sc, sl st into next sc, 1sc into each of next 3 sts, sl st into next sc, berry st into next sc; rep from * to last 2 sts, sl st into next sl st, 1sc into last st, turn.

12th row: 1ch, skip first st, 1sc into next sl st, sl st into next berry st, *1sc into each of next 5 sts, sl st into next berry st, 1sc into next sl st **, sl st into next berry st; rep from *, ending last rep at **, 1sc into last st, turn.

13th and 14th rows: As 9th and 10th rows.

Rep 3rd through 14th rows.

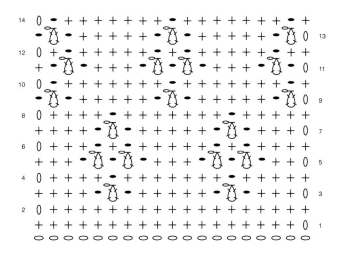

🧅 Berry

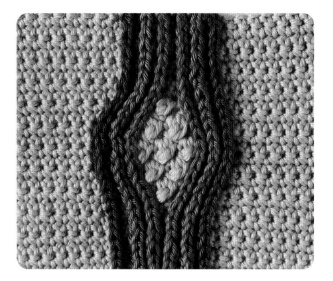

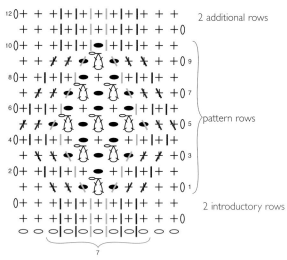

Aran Style II

Worked over 7 sts on a background of basic single crochet with any number of sts.

For berry st, see Aran Style I (page 250).

1st patt row: 1sc into each of next 2 sts, sl st into next st, berry st into next st, sl st into next st, 1sc into each of next 2 sts.

2nd row: 1sc into each of next 3 sts, sl st into next st, 1sc into each of next 3 sts.

3rd row: 1sc into next st, (sl st into next st, berry st into next st) twice, sl st into next st, 1sc into next st.

4th row: 1sc into each of next 2 sts, (sl st into next st, 1sc into next st) twice, 1sc into next st.

5th row: Sl st into next st, (berry st into next st, sl st into next st) 3 times.

6th row: 1sc into next st, (sl st into next st, 1sc into next st) 3 times.

7th and 8th rows: As 3rd and 4th rows.

9th and 10th rows: As 1st and 2nd rows.

Rep 1st through 10th rows. Complete the design by working the lines in raised single crochet from the chart.

0+ + +|+|+|+|+|+|+ + +
+ + +|+|+|+|+|+|+ + +0   2 additional rows

14 0+ + +|+|+|●|+|+|+ + +
+ + ⤢ ⤢ ⤡ ⥮ ⤠ ⤢ ⤡ ⤡ + +0 13

12 0+ +|+|+|● + ●|+|+|+ +
+ ⤢ ⤢ ⤡ ⥮ ● ⤡ ⥮ ⤠ ⤡ ⤡ +0 11

10 0+|+|+|● + ● + ●|+|+|+
+|+|● ⥮ ● ⤠ ● ⥮|● ●|+|+|+0 9

8 0+|+|+|● + ● + ●|+|+|+
+|+|+|● ⥮ ● ⥮ ●|+|+|+|+0 7

6 0+|+|+|● + ● + ●|+|+|+
+|+|● ⥮ ● ⤠ ● ⥮|● ●|+|+|+0 5

4 0+|+|+|+ ● + ● +|+|+|+
+ ⤡ ⤡ ⤠ ⥮ ● ⥮ ⤡ ⤢ ⤢ +0 3

2 0+ +|+|+|+ ● +|+|+|+ +
+ + ⤡ ⤡ ⤡ ⥮ ⤠ ⤢ ⤢ ⤢ + +0 1

0+ + +|+|+|+|+|+|+ + +
+ + +|+|+|+|+|+|+ + +0   2 introductory rows

○ ○ ○ ○|○|○|○|○|○|○ ○ ○ ○

7

pattern rows

Aran Style III

Work in the same way as Aran Style II (page 252). Repeat
1st–6th patt rows, 3rd–6th, 3rd–4th and then 1st and 2nd
rows. Use the chart to work the lines of raised double
crochet.

Uneven Berry Stitch

Multiple of 2 sts.

1st row: Work 1sc into 3rd ch from hook, 1sc into each ch to end, turn.

2nd row: 1ch to count as first sl st, skip first st, *yo and insert hook into next st, yo and draw through a loop, yo and draw through first loop on hook, yo and insert hook into same st, yo and draw through a loop, yo and draw through all 5 loops on hook, 1ch to secure st (Berry st), sl st into next st; rep from * ending with last sl st worked into tch, turn.

3rd row: 1ch to count as first sc, skip first st, *sl st into next berry st, 1sc into next sl st, rep from * to end, turn.

4th row: 1ch to count as first berry st, sl st into next sl st, *1 berry st into next sc, sl st into next sl st, rep from * to last st, sl st in last st, turn.

5th row: 1ch, skip first st, *1sc into next sl st, sl st into next berry st; rep from * to end, turn.

Rep 2nd through 5th rows.

Berry

Colorful Stripes

Multiple of 5 sts.

1st row: Using A, 1 sc in 2nd ch from hook and in each ch to end, turn.

2nd, 3rd, and 4th row: 1 ch, 1 sc in first sc and in each sc to end., turn but at end of Row 4, draw B through last 2 loops of last sc, turn.

5th row: 1 ch, 1 sc in first sc and in each of next 3 sc, *working in row below draw up loop in sc below sc just worked and in each of next 2 sc, insert hook in next sc of 4th row and draw yarn through sc and 3 loops, yo and through remaining 2 loops (cluster), 1 sc in each of next 4 sc; rep from * to end, turn.

6th row: 1 ch, 1 sc in first sc and in each st to end, drawing A through 2 loops of last sc, turn.

Rep 3rd through 6th row.

Other crochet stitches, such as slip stitch or double crochet, may be substituted instead of the raised single crochet, depending on the depth of stitch required.

 Cluster

Loop Stitch

Any number of sts.

1st row: 1sc into 3rd ch from hook, work 1sc into every ch to end, turn.

2nd row: 1ch to count as first sc, skip first st , work a loop by inserting hook into next st, position yarn over 1st and 2nd fingers and extend yarn by lifting 2nd finger, draw through a loop, then draw loop through st, yo and draw through both loops on hook, remove 2nd finger from loop, rep the action of making a loop into every st to the end of the row, 1sc into the turning chain. Turn.

3rd row: 1ch, skip first st, 1sc into every st to end, 1sc into the tch. Turn.

Rep 2nd and 3rd rows.

Note: The loops are on the back of the fabric as you are working. The density of the loops can be altered by working them across the row on alternate stitches, and into the stitches between loops on following alternate rows.

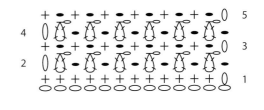

Even Berry Stitch

Multiple of 2 sts.

1st row: Work 1sc into 3rd ch from hook, 1sc into each ch to end, turn.

2nd row: 1ch (count as first sl st), skip first st, *yo and insert hook into next st, yo and draw through a loop, yo and draw through first loop on hook, yo and insert hook into same st, yo and draw through a loop, yo and draw through all 5 loops on hook, 1ch to secure st (Berry st), sl st into next st; rep from * ending with last sl st worked into turning ch, turn.

3rd row: 1ch (count as first sc), skip first st, *sl st into next berry st, 1sc into next sl st; rep from * to end, turn.

4th row: 1ch to count as first sl st, *1 berry st into next sl st, sl st into next sc; rep from * to end, turn.

Rep 3rd and 4th rows.

Berry

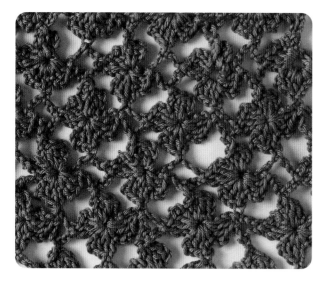

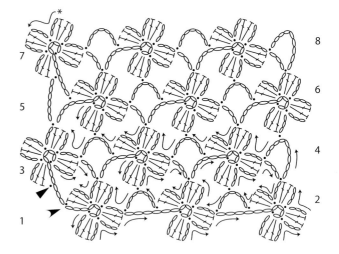

Floral Trellis Stitch

Any number of sts.

1st row (RS): 7ch, *sl st into 4th ch from hook, 3ch, into ring just formed work a Base Flower Unit of [2dc, 3ch, sl st, 3ch, 2dc]**, 10ch; rep from * ending last rep at ** when fabric is required width, then keep same side facing and turn so as to be able to work along underside of Base Flower Units.

2nd row (RS): *3ch, sl st into ch ring at center of Flower, 3ch, [2dc, 3ch, sl st—center Petal completed, 3ch, 2dc] all into same ring, skip 2ch of base chain that connects Units, sl st into next ch**, 7ch, skip 2ch, sl st into next ch; rep from * into next and each Base Flower Unit to end, ending at **, turn. **Note:** Check that each Base Flower Unit is not twisted before you work into it.

3rd row: 10ch, sl st into 4th ch from hook, 3ch, 2dc into ring just formed, 3ch, sl st into top of 3ch of center Petal of last Flower made in previous row (see diagram), *10ch, sl st into 4th ch from hook, 3ch, 2dc into ring just formed, sl st into 4th of next 7ch arch of previous row, 3ch, [sl st, 3ch, 2dc] into same ch ring as last 2dc, 3ch, sl st into top of 3ch of center Petal of next Flower in previous row; rep from * to end, turn.

4th row: 9ch, skip 2ch, sl st into next ch, *3ch, sl st into ch ring at center of Flower, 3ch, work [2dc, 3ch, sl st, 3ch, 2dc] into same ring, skip 2ch, sl st into next ch, 7ch, skip [3ch, sl st and next 2ch], sl st into next ch; rep from * ending 3ch, sl st into ch ring at center of last Flower, 3ch, 2dc into same ring, turn.

5th row: *10ch, sl st into 4th ch from hook, 3ch, 2dc into ring just formed, sl st into 4th ch of next arch of previous row, 3ch, [sl st, 3ch, 2dc] into same ch ring as last 2dc**, 3ch, sl st into top of 3ch of center Petal of next Flower in previous row; rep from * ending last rep at **, turn.

6th row: *3ch, sl st into ch ring at center of Flower, 3ch, [2dc, 3ch, sl st, 3ch, 2dc] all into same ring, skip 2ch, sl st into next ch**, 7ch, skip [3ch, sl st, 2ch], sl st into next ch; rep from *, ending last rep at **.

Rep 3rd to 6th rows.

When fabric is required length, finishing after a 4th (RS) row (see * on diagram), cont down left side to complete edge Flowers as follows: *3ch, [sl st, 3ch, 2dc, 3ch, sl st, 3ch, 2dc] all into ch ring at center of edge Flower, skip 3ch, sl st into next ch**, 6ch, sl st into last ch before center Petal of next edge Flower (see diagram); rep from * ending last rep at ** after last edge Flower.

Fasten off.

Cut Fur Stitch

Odd number of sts.

1st row: 1sc into 3rd ch from hook, *1ch, skip next ch, 1sc into next ch; rep from * to end. Turn.

2nd row: 1ch to count as first sc, 1sc into first 1ch sp, *1ch, 1sc into next ch sp; rep from * to last sp, 1ch, 1sc into the turning chain, turn.

Rep 2nd row.

To add the loops, cut lengths of yarn as required (approximately 5in/12.5cm long).

Take two pieces of yarn together each time and fold in half, with RS of work facing, insert crochet hook through the first sc in the mesh, place the two loops of yarn over the hook and draw through the work, place the four cut ends of yarn over the hook, and draw through the two loops on the hook. Pull tight to secure. Repeat.

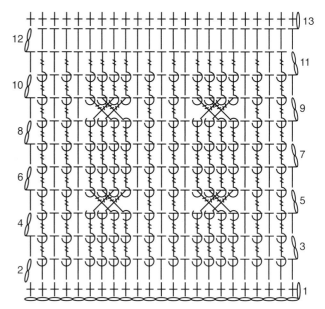

Four-Stitch Cable Afghan

Panel of 23 sts.

(add 1 for base ch).

Special Abbreviations: Front Post Triple (fptr) = Yarn over hook twice, insert hook from front to back around the post of the stitch to be worked, yarn over hook, pull up a loop, then: (yarn over hook, draw yarn through two loops on hook) three times. In this pattern, the stitch behind the fptr is to be skipped.

Back Post Triple (bptr) = Yarn over hook twice, insert hook from back to front around the post of the stitch to be worked, yarn over hook, pull up a loop, then: (yarn over hook, draw yarn through two loops on hook) three times. In this pattern, the stitch behind the bptr is to be skipped.

1st row: Sc in 2nd ch from hook. Sc in each ch. (23 sc).

2nd row: Ch 2 (counts as first hdc), hdc in each sc. (23 hdc).

3rd row: Ch 2 (counts as first hdc), *(fptr in next st, hdc in next st) twice, fptr in each of next 4 sts, hdc in next st; rep from * once, (fptr in next st, hdc in next st) twice.

4th row: Ch 2 (counts as first hdc), *(bptr in next st, hdc in next st) twice, bptr in each of next 4 sts, hdc in next st; rep from * once, (bptr in next st, hdc in next st) twice.

5th row: Ch 2 (counts as first hdc), (fptr in next st, hdc in next st) twice, *skip next 2 sts, fptr in each of next 2 sts; next, working in front of the 2 sts just worked, fptr in each of the 2 skipped sts, hdc in next st, (fptr in next st, hdc in next st) twice; rep from * one time.

6th row: Work as row 4.

7th row: Work as row 3.

8th row: Work as row 4.

9th row: Work as row 5.

10th row: Work as row 4.

11th row: Work as row 3.

12th row: Ch 2 (counts as first hdc), hdc in each st across. (23 hdc).

13th Row: Ch 1, sc in each hdc across. Do not fasten off.

Finishing rnd: Ch 1, working down outside edge of rows: sc in end of the sc row, (2 sc around post of the end hdc of next row) 11 times altogether, sc in end of the sc row, ch 1, sc in same stitch as sc just made, sc in each st across bottom row until you reach the last sc. (sc, ch 1, sc) in last sc of bottom row. Next, working along other side: (2 sc around post of the end hdc of next row) 11 times altogether. (sc, ch 1, sc) in end of sc row. Sc in each st across top row. Sl st in first sc of this round to join. Fasten off. Weave in ends.

Creating a textured crochet afghan is quite easy. Combine stitches, create wonderful textured effects, and work them in your favorite colors to create an heirloom from generation to generation.

Arrow Pattern

Multiple of 4 sts + 1.

1st row: 1sc into 2nd ch from hook, 1sc into each ch, turn.

2nd row: 1ch, skip first sc, 1sc into each sc, turn.

3rd row: 3ch, skip first sc, 1dc into next sc, *skip 3sc, 1dtr into next sc, 1dc into each of 3 skipped sc (working behind dtr); rep from * to last 2 sts, 1dc into each of last 2sc, turn.

4th row: 3ch, skip 1dc, 1dc into next dc, * skip 3dc, 1dtr into dtr, 1dc into each of 3 skipped dc (working in front of dtr); rep from * ending 1dc into each of last 2dc, turn.

5th row: 1ch, skip 1dc, 1sc into each remaining dc, turn.

Rep 2nd through 5th rows.

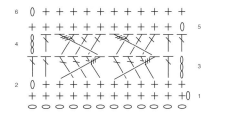

key

Stitch diagrams are detailed "maps" of fabric as viewed from the right side. They enable you to see what you are going to do before you start and also where you are at any moment.

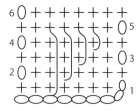

Spikes: The stitch symbol is extended downward to show where the hook is to go through the fabric.

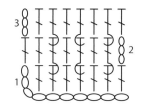

Raised (relief) stitches: When a stitch is to be worked by inserting the hook behind a stem (instead of under the top two loops), the stitch symbol ends in a "crook" around the appropriate stem. The direction of the crook indicates which side of the fabric the hook is to be inserted. On a RS row, work a raised stitch with a RS crook at the front, and one with a left crook at the back.

Back/front loop: Stitches that are to be made by inserting the hook under only one of the top two loops are indicated by heavy and lightweight stitch symbols with underlining. A lightweight symbol in conjunction with an underline means pick up the loop nearest the right side of the fabric, i.e. front loop on right-side rows, but back loop on wrong-side rows. A heavyweight symbol with an underline means pick up the loop nearest the wrong-side, i.e. back loop on right-side rows, but front loop on wrong-side rows.

Distortion: Stitch symbols are drawn and laid out realistically, but are distorted for the sake of clarity. Sometimes, for example, single crochet stitches may look extra long. This is only to show clearly where they go and you should not to make artificially long stitches.

When the diagram represents a fabric that is not intended to lie flat—for instance, a "gathered" or frilled edging—since the drawing itself has to remain flat, the stitch symbols have to be stretched.

Chain

Slip Stitch

+

Single Crochet

Half Double Crochet

Double Crochet

Treble

Double Treble

Triple Treble

Quadruple Treble

Quintuple Treble

Bullion Stitch

Lace Loop

Solomon's Knot

2   3

Single Crochet Cluster

2   3   3   4   5

Half Double Crochet Cluster

2   3   3   4   5

Double Crochet Cluster

Treble Cluster

2   3   5   9

Double Treble Cluster

Marguerites = the individual parts of the marguerite clusters have barbs.

3   4

Popcorns: Half Double Treble

3   4   5

Popcorns: Double Crochet

5   7

Popcorns: Treble

1   1   2   2

Crossed Stitches

'X' Shape

+ + + + + + + +

Picots = when a single picot loop occurs after a solid stitch, note the usual method of working the closing slip stitch.

Figures = figures indicate row (or round) numbers.

Color = letters A, B, etc, and also light and heavy stitch symbols confirm changes of color.

Arrows = once you are familiar with the basic fabric-making procedures, it is usually clear where a stitch pattern diagram begins and ends, which direction a row goes, etc (Hint: Look for the turning chain). If there is any doubt, additional directions are given with the help of various arrows.

◀ Commence

◁ Re-join yarn

◀ Bind off

← Direction of row

2, 3, and 4 Half Double Crochet Group = work 2 (3, 4) half double crochet into same place.

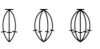

2, 3, 4 and 5 Double Crochet Group = work 2 (3, 4, 5) double crochet into same place.

2, 3, 4 and 5 Treble Group = work 2 (3, 4, 5) treble into same place.

3, 4, and 5 Double Crochet Cluster = work a double crochet into each of the next 3 (4, 5) stitches leaving the last loop of each on the hook. Yarn over and draw through all loops on hook.

3, 4, and 5 Treble Cluster = work a treble into each of the next 3 (4, 5) stitches, leaving the last loop of each on the hook. Yarn over and draw through all loops on hook.

3, 4, and 5 Double Crochet bobble = follow instructions as if working a cluster but for each "leg" insert the hook into the same stitch or space. For a Five Dc Bobble, work five double crochet into one stitch leaving the last loop of each on the hook. Yarn over and draw through all the loops on the hook. More bulky bobbles can be secured with an extra chain stitch. If this is necessary it would be necessary it would be indicated within the pattern.

4, 5, 6, and 7 Treble Bobble = follow instructions as if working a cluster but for each "leg" insert the hook into the same stitch or space.

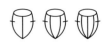

Five Dc Popcorn = work five double crochet into one stitch. Take the hook out of the working loop and insert it into the top of the first double crochet made, from front to back. Pick up the working loop and draw this through to close the popcorn. If required work one chain to secure the popcorn. On diagrams the point at the base of the popcorn will be positioned above the space or stitch where it is to be worked.

3 and 4 Half Double crochet popcorn = work 3 (4) half double crochet into the same place, drop loop off hook, insert hook into first half double crochet, pick up dropped loop and draw through.

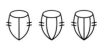

3, 4, and 5 Double Crochet Popcorn = work 3 (4, 5) double crochet into the same place, drop loop off hook, insert hook into first double crochet, pick up dropped loop and draw through.

3, 4, and 5 Treble Popcorn = work 3 (4, 5) treble into the same place, drop loop off hook, insert hook into first treble, pick up dropped loop and draw through.

Three Half Double Crochet Puff Stitch =

Work 3 half double crochet into same stitch, leaving the last 2 loops of each on the hook. Yarn over and draw through all loops on hook. If required, work one chain to secure the puff stitch.

Crossed Treble = Skip

two stitches and work the first treble into next stitch. Work one chain then work second treble into first of skipped stitches taking the hook behind the first treble before inserting. See individual pattern instructions for variations on crossed stitch.

Four Chain Picot =

(Closed with a slip stitch). Work four chains. Into fourth chain from hook work a slip stitch to close. Continue working chain or required stitch.

abbreviations

Most crochet pattern instructions are written out in words. In order to follow these, you must be able to understand the simple jargon, abbreviations, and standard conventions.

alt = alternate

approx = approximate(ly)

beg = begin(ning)

ch sp = chain space

ch(s) = chain(s)

CL = cluster

cm = centimeter(s)

cont = continue

dc = double crochet

dec = decrease

dtr = double treble

foll = follows

gr = group

hdc = half double crochet

inc = increase

prev = previous

quad tr = quadruple treble

quin tr = quintuple treble

rem = remaining

rep = repeat

RS = right side

sc = single crochet

sl st = slip stitch

st(s) = stitch(es)

stch = starting chain

tch = turning chain

tog = together

tr = treble

ttr = triple treble

WS = wrong side

yo = yarn over

Jargon Busting

Base (foundation) chain

The length of chain made at the beginning of a piece of crochet as a basis for constructing the fabric.

Turning/starting chain

One or more chains, depending upon the length of stitch required, worked at the beginning of a row (or end of the previous row) as preparation for the new row; sometimes counts as the first stitch in the new row. Called "starting chain" when working "in the round."

Group

Several stitches worked into the same place; sometimes called "shell," "fan," etc.

Picot

A run of chain stitches normally brought back on itself and fixed into a decorative loop with a slip stitch or single crochet. **Note:** Terms such as "group," "cluster," "picot," and even "shell," "fan," "flower," "petal," "leaf," "bobble," etc, do not denote a fixed arrangement of stitches. Exactly what they mean may be different for each pattern. The procedure is therefore always spelled out at the beginning of each set of instructions and is valid only for that set, unless stated otherwise.

Yarn over

The stitch-making instruction to wrap the yarn from the ball over the hook (or manipulate the hook around the yarn) in order to make a new loop; always done in a counterclockwise direction, unless otherwise stated.

Work straight

Work over an existing row of stitches without "increasing" (i.e. adding stitches and so making the fabric wider), or "decreasing" (i.e. reducing the number of stitches and so making the fabric narrower). Precise methods of increasing and decreasing vary according to each stitch pattern and circumstances and are detailed in pattern instructions.

Front/back

"Front" and "back" mean the front and back surfaces of a fabric for the time being as you hold and look at it; these change over every time you turn the work. **Note:** In garment pattern instructions, the terms "front" and "back" denote the different pieces of the garment.

Multiple

All but the simplest crochet stitch patterns are built around repeated sequences of stitches. In order to make sense of the instructions, you must have exactly the right number of stitches in your base row is also given. This number is a multiple of the number of stitches required for one complete sequence—sometimes plus an extra edge stitch or two—and is given at the beginning of each set of instructions.

The number of chains you need for the base chain, in order to be able to create the appropriate number of stitches in the base row, is also given. For example, "Multiple of 2 sts + 1, (add 1 for base chain)" = make 4, 6, 8, etc chains for a base row of 3, 5, 7, etc, stitches; or "Multiple of 8 sts + 3, (add 2 for base chain)" = make 13, 21, 29, etc, chains for a base row of 11, 19, 27, etc, stitches.

Color

Capital letters A, B, C, D, etc are used to indicate different yarn colors; when only two colors are involved and one of these is intended to dominate, the terms "main (M)" and "contrast (C)" may be used instead.

Asterisks (*) and Brackets [ ]

These are used to simplify repetition. Instructions are put inside brackets and these are to be worked the number of times stated, for example: "[1ch, skip 1ch, 1dc into next st] 5 times."

A sequence of stitches after an asterisk means that the whole sequence between that asterisk and the next semi-colon is to be repeated as many times as necessary to reach the end of the row, for example:

"*1ch, skip 1ch, 1dc into next st, 1ch, skip 1ch, 1dc into each of next 3 sts; rep from * to end, turn."

If no further details are given, as in this case, the end of the sequence will coincide exactly with the end of the row. If there are stitches remaining unworked after the last complete repeat sequence, details of how to complete the row are given, for example: "Rep from * to last 4 sts, ending 1ch, skip 1ch, 1dc into each of last 3 sts, turn." "Rep from * 4 more times," means work that sequence 5 times in all.

Stitch Diagrams

Accurate stitch diagrams show the overall picture at a glance and at the same time indicate precisely every detail of construction. To follow them you need to be familiar with the symbols that represent each individual stitch. Stitch diagrams have been provided for most stitches, depending on the level of complexity.

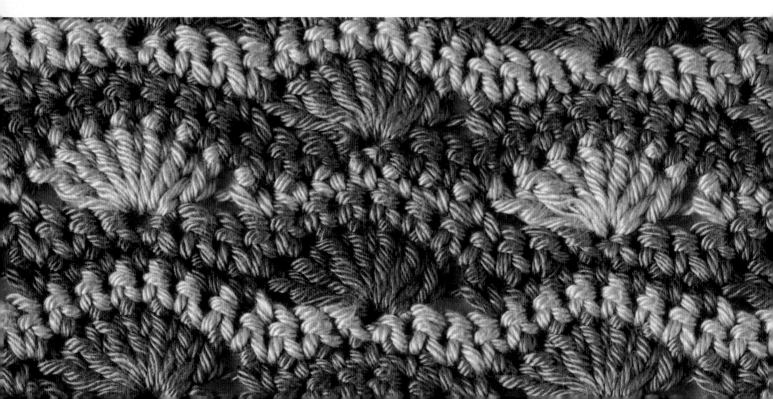

index

resources

Rowan

Westminster Fibers, Inc

3, Northern Boulevard

Suite 3

Amherst

NH 03031

www.westminsterfibers.com

Other titles currently available in the Harmony Guides series:

CROCHET   KNIT

Publisher's Acknowledgements

First and foremost, we'd like to thank Rowan Yarns for suppplying all the yarns used throughout this book. We would like to thank all those who helped recreate the swatches: Heather Stephenson, Melina Kalatzi, Sharon Brant and her team of crocheters. Lastly, we would like to thank all past and present editors who have contributed to the series. All photography by Michael Wicks.

Interweave Crochet is your single best source for crochet news, ideas, articles, and best of all — patterns! www.interweavecrochet.com

INTERWEAVE
CROCHET